Key Stage 3

Dev[illegible]lop[illegible]

NUMBERS AND THE NUMBER SYSTEM

ACTIVITIES FOR TEACHING NUMERACY

year 7

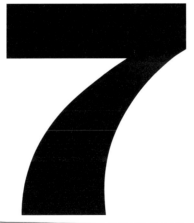

Hilary Koll and Steve Mills

A & C BLACK

Contents

Published 2003 by A & C Black Publishers Limited
37 Soho Square, London W1D 3QZ
www.acblack.com

ISBN 0-7136-6465-7

Editors: Lynne Williamson and Marie Lister

The authors and publishers would like to thank David Chadwick, Corinne McCrum and Jane McNeill for their advice in producing this series of books.

A CIP catalogue record for this book is available from the British Library.

Printed in Great Britain by St Edmundsbury Press Ltd, Bury St Edmunds, Suffolk.

A & C Black uses paper produced with elemental chlorine-free pulp, harvested from managed sustainable forests.

Introduction

Key Stage 3 **Developing Numeracy: Numbers and the Number System** is a series of photocopiable resources for Years 7, 8 and 9, designed to be used during maths lessons. The books focus on the Numbers and the Number System strand of the Key Stage 3 National Strategy *Framework for teaching mathematics.*

Each book supports the teaching of mathematics by providing a series of activities that develop essential skills in numeracy. The activities aim to reinforce learning and develop the skills and understanding explored during whole-class teaching. Each task provides practice and consolidation of an objective contained in the framework document. On the whole the activities are designed for pupils to work on independently, either individually or in pairs, although occasionally some pupils may need support.

The activities in **Numbers and the Number System Year 7** relate to the following topics:

- place value, ordering and rounding;
- integers, powers and roots;
- fractions, decimals, percentages, ratio and proportion.

How to use this book

Each double-page spread is based around a Year 7 objective. The spread has three main sections labelled A, B and C, and ends with a challenge (**Now try this!**). The work grows increasingly difficult from A through to C, and the 'Now try this!' challenge reinforces and extends pupils' learning. The activities provide the teacher with an opportunity to make informal assessments: for example, checking that pupils are developing mental strategies, have grasped the main teaching points, or whether they have any misunderstandings.

This double-page structure can be used in a variety of ways: for example, following whole-class teaching the pupils can begin to work through both sheets and will experience gradually more complex questions, or the teacher can choose the most appropriate starting points for each group in the class, with some pupils starting at A and others at B or C. This allows differentiation for mixed-ability groups. 'Now try this!' provides a greater challenge for more able pupils. It can involve 'Using and Applying' concepts and skills, and provides an opportunity for classroom discussion. Where appropriate, pupils can be asked to finish tasks for homework.

The instructions are presented clearly to enable pupils to work independently. There are also opportunities for pupils to work in pairs and groups, to encourage discussion and co-operation. A calculator icon indicates parts of the activities where the pupils will need to use calculators. Where there is no icon, the teacher or pupils may choose whether or not to use them. Brief notes are provided at the foot of each page to assist the pupil or classroom assistant, or parent if the sheets are used for homework. Remind the pupils to read these before beginning the activity.

In some cases, the pupils will need to record their workings on a separate piece of paper, and it is suggested that these workings are handed in with the activity sheets. The pupils will also need to record their answers to some of the 'Now try this!' challenges on another piece of paper.

Organisation

Very little equipment is needed, other than the essential rulers, pencils and so on. Some activity sheets involve the use of calculators; these activities allow opportunities for pupils to explore keys and interpret the display on the calculator, considering issues such as rounding. During the teaching input, ensure that the pupils understand the functions of the various calculator keys they will be using.

To help teachers select appropriate learning experiences for pupils, the activities are grouped into sections within the book to match the objectives in the Key Stage 3 National Strategy *Yearly teaching programmes*. However, the activities do not have to be used in the order given. The sheets are intended to support, rather than direct, the teacher's planning.

Some activities can be made easier or more challenging by masking or substituting some of the numbers. You may wish to re-use some pages by copying them onto card and laminating them, or by enlarging them onto A3 paper. They could also be made into OHTs for whole-class use.

Teachers' notes

Further brief notes, containing specific instructions or points to be raised during the first part of the lesson, are provided for particular sheets (see pages 6–7).

Whole-class oral and mental starters

The following activities provide some practical ideas to support the main teaching part of the lesson, and can be carried out before pupils use the activity sheets.

Place value, ordering and rounding

Get in line

Draw a number line on the board, marked with ten equal divisions. (It may be useful to have a large number line like this laminated for regular use.) Choose two integers or decimals to write at each end of the line, for example 0 and 1000 or 0.6 and 0.7. Invite pupils to come to the board and to write in the number for each division on the line, for example 100, 200, 300... or 0.61, 0.62, 0.63... Encourage pupils to find the difference between the two end numbers and to divide this by ten to find the size of each interval.

Round and round

Use digit cards to show a large number, for example 53 473. Ask pupils to round the number. When they begin to answer, point out that you need to tell them to what level to round: for example to the nearest 10, 100, 1000 or 10 000. Call out one level, e.g. *to the nearest 100*, and invite them to give the answer. Repeat for other levels. Then use the digit cards to create a new number and repeat the activity. Introduce decimals at an appropriate stage and discuss language such as 'to the nearest tenth' and 'to 1 decimal place'.

Integers, powers and roots

Show me

Give each pupil two sets of 0–9 digit cards. Play 'show me' activities, for example: *Show me a square number between 72 and 99*; *Show me a multiple of 14 greater than 45*; *Show me he highest two-digit prime number*. Pupils 'show' a number by holding one or two digit cards in the air.

Common factors

Split the class into two teams (A and B). Write two numbers on the board, for example 36 and 48. Ask Team A to list all the factors of each number and then to find the common factors of the two numbers. The team scores a point for each common factor they find. In this example, the factors of 36 are 1, 2, 3, 4, 6, 9, 12, 18, 36; the factors of 48 are 1, 2, 3, 4, 6, 8, 12, 16, 24, 48; so 1, 2, 3, 4, 6 and 12 are the common factors. Team A would score six points if they found them all. Repeat for Team B, using two different numbers.

Fractions, decimals, percentages, ratio and proportion

Order, order

Invite up to ten pupils to the front. Give each pupil a fraction or a decimal card. The pupils should face the class and hold the cards in front of them. Ask the pupils to order themselves from highest to lowest. Mixing fractions and decimals can prompt useful discussion, for example $\frac{1}{2}$, 0.35, 0.4, $\frac{2}{3}$, 0.85.

Percentages

Split the class into up to five teams. Write five percentages across the board in increasing size, for example 10%, 25%, 40%, 75%, 90%. Beneath each percentage write a number decreasing in size, for example 180, 120, 90, 88, 50. Use these as five different percentage questions (10% of 180, 25% of 120, and so on). Ask each team to choose one question that they think has the highest value. They should then find the values of all five percentages. The team (or teams) with the highest value scores a point.

Proportions

On the board, list pairs of numbers with the same proportions, for example 5 ➔ 35, 2 ➔ 14, and 6 ➔ 42. Ask pupils to find other pairs of numbers within the same proportional set and to describe how the numbers are related (in this example, multiplying the first number by 7). Ask pupils to find the second number when given the first, for example 1 ➔ ? (7) and 9 ➔ ? (63). Discuss how the first number can be found from the second (÷ 7). Give some examples of second numbers and ask pupils to find the first numbers, for example ? ← 49 (7) and ? ← 77 (11).

Teachers' notes

Place value, ordering and rounding

Pages 8 & 9

During the teaching input, revise column headings for numbers to one million. Discuss how, when writing large numbers, we group digits in threes from the right-hand side, and how commas are sometimes used to show these groups. In part C, some pupils may require assistance with spelling; a wall chart would be a useful aid.

Pages 10 & 11

A useful starter activity could involve counting in steps of one-tenth or one-hundredth from any number, for example 4.3, 4.4, 4.5, 4.6... This could be as a whole class or counting around the room. Revise column headings for decimals to three decimal places.

Pages 12 & 13

Avoid describing the effect of multiplying by ten as 'add a nought', as this does not apply to decimals and can confuse some pupils when adding zero to a number. Instead, describe the effect as the digits moving across one column to the left. Discuss how dividing by 10 or 100 can be described in different ways, for example finding one tenth or one hundredth of a number, or finding 10% or 1% of a number. More able pupils can be introduced to the idea that multiplying by 0.1 has the same effect as dividing by 10.

Pages 14 & 15

Pupils may previously have encountered or developed the idea that multiplying by 10 can be done by 'adding a nought'. This strategy does not apply to multiplying decimals, so pupils will need to be shown how the digits move across the columns. Draw columns on the board and stick digit cards in place. Invite pupils to come to the front and move the digits, adding zeros as 'place holders' where necessary, for example $6.1 \times 1000 = 6100$. Encourage pupils to make approximations at all times: for example, this is about 6×1000, so the answer must be about 6000.

Pages 16 & 17

A useful starter activity could involve exploring decimals on a number line, drawn either on the board or on a computer. Encourage pupils to suggest numbers that lie between two of the numbers shown. Discuss how, when comparing decimals, it sometimes helps to add zero(s) so that all the decimals have the same number of decimal places: for example, to compare 4.5 and 4.37, write them as 4.50 and 4.37.

Pages 18 & 19

Revise rounding strategies paying attention to the convention of 5, 50, 500 and so on rounding up rather than down. In part C, pupils are required to make their own decisions about to what level to round numbers in real-life contexts. Discuss the way in which numbers are rounded in newspaper headlines: for example, *20 000 people attended concert, £3 million won on lottery*.

Pages 20 & 21

Rounding is an essential skill when interpreting calculator displays. When dividing, an answer may have many decimal places. Discuss how each digit is less significant than the digit to its left. For example in the number 34, the digit 3 representing thirty is more significant than the digit 4 representing 4 units. We sometimes round so that we only give the most significant information: for example, rather than writing 374.5628406 we might put 374.6 or 375.

Integers, powers and roots

Pages 22 & 23

Before the pupils begin the activity, revise the term 'integer' to mean a positive or negative whole number (including zero). Remind pupils of the 'greater than' and 'less than' signs and point out that, like a greedy mouth, the wider part opens towards the larger number. For part C, some pupils may need further input on coordinates in all four quadrants.

Pages 24 & 25

The idea of adding or subtracting a negative number is a difficult one (see part C). Rather than just teaching a rule, spend some time discussing how to subtract a debt, i.e. to add the amount owed: for example, *You owe me £10. You want to get rid of your debt (subtract a negative), so you must pay that amount to me (add it)*. Such contexts can help pupils to understand a reason for the rule, and also help them to remember it more effectively.

Pages 26 & 27

Ensure pupils understand that a factor is a number that divides exactly into another: for example, 5 is a factor of 20 as it divides exactly into 20 without a remainder. Introduce the idea that factors can often be found in pairs. For example, if you know that 5 is a factor of 20 and you know that $5 \times 4 = 20$, then 4 is also a factor. Write a number on the board, e.g. 36. Explain that 1 and the number itself are always factors. Then consider the number 2. Is 2 a factor of 36? If it is, ask by which number it can be multiplied to get 36 (18). Write these two numbers as a pair. Then move on to the number 3 and its pair 12, and so on until all the factors are listed: 1 and 36, 2 and 18, 3 and 12, 4 and 9, and 6. Explain that sometimes a factor is paired with itself (such as 6 and 6) so we only need write it as a factor once.

Pages 28 & 29

Introduce the term 'lowest common multiple' during the first part of the lesson. Remind pupils that a multiple is a number in a particular times table, or beyond. For example, 60 is a multiple of 3. If you continued the 3 times table, it would eventually reach 60. Explain that a 'common multiple' is a number in more than one times table: for example, 20 is a common multiple of 2, 4, 5 and 10 as it's in all these times tables.

Write the numbers 6 and 4 on the board. Ask pupils to state some multiples of each number. Ask them to identify the common multiples (12, 24, 36, 48 ...) and to find the lowest one.

Pages 30 & 31

During the first part of the lesson, find out which tests of divisibility the pupils already know: for example, *a number is divisible by 9 if the sum of its digits is a multiple of 9.* Discuss other tests of divisibility and write numbers on the board for the pupils to test.

Fractions, decimals, percentages, ratio and proportion

Pages 36 & 37

Remind pupils of the conventions of writing fractions: the denominator (the number on the bottom) shows the number of equal parts into which the whole has been divided and the numerator (the number on the top) shows the number of these parts being considered. Explain that you can describe one number as a fraction of another: for example, 25cm out of one metre (100cm) can be expressed as $\frac{25}{100}$ and then simplified to $\frac{1}{4}$. Show pupils how equivalent fractions can be written by dividing (or multiplying) the numerator and the denominator by the same number. For example, $\frac{5}{15}$ is equivalent to $\frac{50}{150}$ (multiplying the numerator and the denominator by 10) or $\frac{1}{3}$ (by dividing both by 5).

Pages 38 & 39

Remind pupils that equivalent fractions have the same value but look different, for example $\frac{1}{4}$ and $\frac{2}{8}$. Demonstrate how equivalent fractions can be written by dividing (or multiplying) the numerator and the denominator by the same number. For example, $\frac{5}{15}$ is equivalent to $\frac{50}{150}$ (multiplying the numerator and the denominator by 10) or $\frac{1}{3}$ (by dividing both by 5).

Ask pupils to generate a 'fraction family' on the board by listing equivalent fractions, for example those equivalent to $\frac{20}{100}$. Point out the fraction in the list formed by the smallest numbers ($\frac{1}{5}$). Explain that this is known as a fraction 'in its simplest form' or 'in its lowest terms'.

Pages 40 & 41

When adding and subtracting fractions, pupils often make the mistake of adding the numerators and the denominators. It is useful to provide visual examples of fractions and to discuss with pupils how this cannot be the case: for example, $\frac{1}{2}$ + $\frac{1}{2}$ cannot equal $\frac{2}{4}$, as $\frac{2}{4}$ is equivalent to $\frac{1}{2}$.

Pages 44 & 45

Once pupils have shaded the straws in part C, the cards can be cut out and arranged in pairs that have the same answer. These pairs could be stuck into a book as a record.

Pages 48 & 49

During the oral and mental starter, practise finding simple percentages of numbers mentally, for example 10% of 120, 50% of 90. Encourage pupils to suggest their own strategies for finding percentages of numbers: for example, to find 75%, halve the number, halve again to find 25%, then multiply 25% by 3; alternatively add the two 'halve' numbers (50% and 25%); alternatively subtract 25% from the original number.

The pupils will need to work in pairs for the game in part C.

Pages 52 & 53

Once pupils have estimated the proportions in part C, they could be given protractors and asked to measure the angles of the sectors of the pie charts. They could then find these as exact percentage proportions of 360° and check their estimates.

Pages 56 & 57

Pupils often experience great difficulty understanding the difference between ratio and proportion. Encourage them to think of proportion as a fraction, decimal or percentage, and of ratio as a comparison between two or more parts of a whole, written using a colon, for example 3 : 2. Ratio compares part with part, while proportion compares a part with the whole. Pupils may need many examples in context before this is fully understood.

Understand and use place value

Enormous integers

A

1. With a partner, take turns to read aloud each number in the grid.
2. On the first line, write the value of the underlined digit in each number.
3. On the second line, write the value of the digit 4 in each number.

Write each value in words and in figures.

	M	HTh	TTh	Th	H	T	U
(a)			5	3	<u>8</u>	2	4
(b)		2	0	1	4	<u>5</u>	9
(c)		1	6	<u>2</u>	3	4	8
(d)		4	<u>7</u>	9	1	0	3
(e)	1	<u>8</u>	4	5	0	5	6
(f)	<u>9</u>	0	7	4	0	0	8

(a) *eight hundred* 800
four 4

(b) ____________________
____

(c) ____________________
____

(d) ____________________
____

(e) ____________________
____

(f) ____________________
____

B

Join the numbers in figures to the numbers in words.

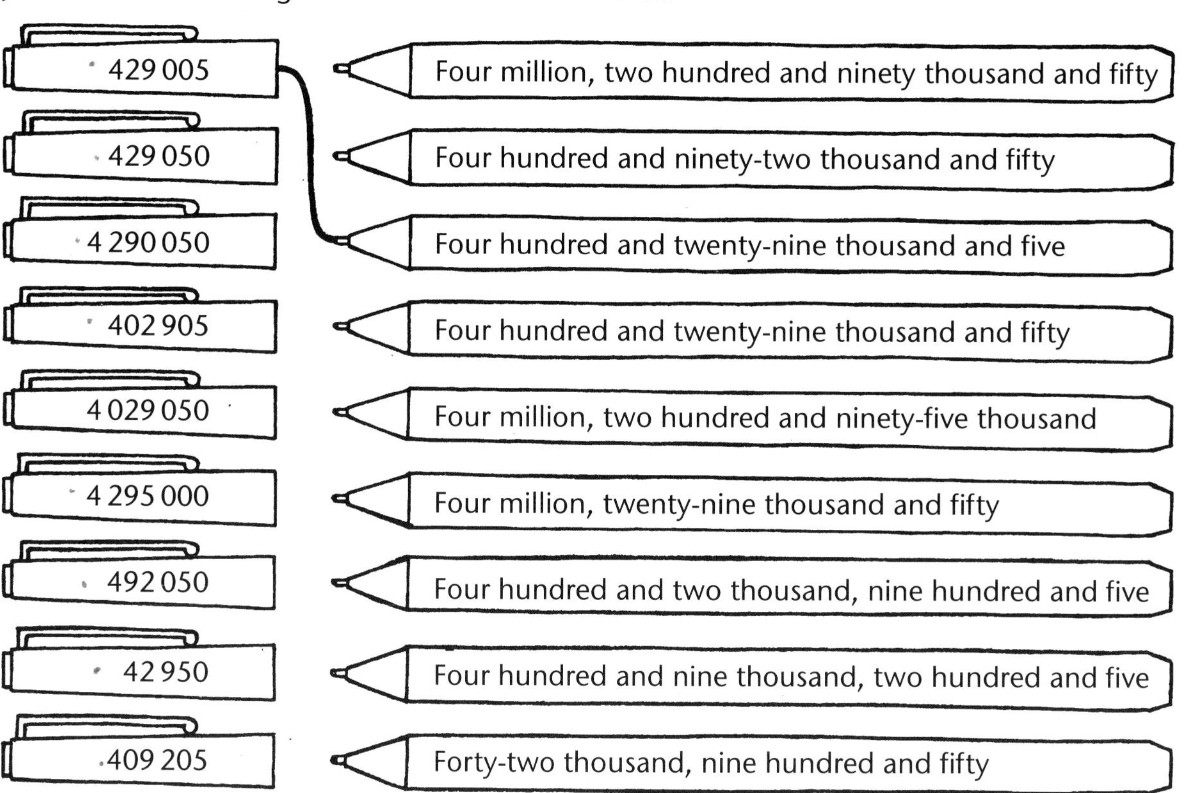

It is important to know what each digit in a number stands for. Make sure you know the column headings as shown in the table above. It sometimes helps to group the digits in threes, starting from the right, for example 1234567 becomes 1 234 567.

Enormous integers

Understand and use place value

These pupils have discovered a pattern in the digits of large numbers. Follow their instructions.

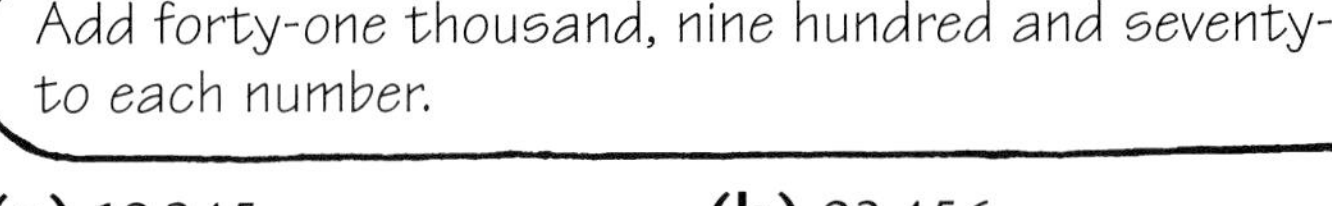

1. *Add forty-one thousand, nine hundred and seventy-six to each number.*

(a) 12 345 **(b)** 23 456 **(c)** 34 567

Answer ________ Answer ________ Answer ________

What do you notice? ________________________

2. *Add five hundred and thirty thousand, eight hundred and sixty-five to each number.*

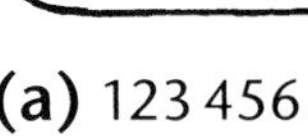

(a) 123 456 **(b)** 234 567 **(c)** 345 678

Answer ________ Answer ________ Answer ________

What do you notice? ________________________

3. Which number can you add to produce the same effect on these numbers? Write the number to be added in words.

Add ________________________ to each number.

(a) 1 234 567 **(b)** 2 345 678 **(c)** 3 456 789

Answer 7 654 321 Answer 8 765 432 Answer 9 876 543

4. Which number can you add to *twelve million, three hundred and forty-five thousand, six hundred and seventy-eight* to reverse the digits? Write the number to be added in words.

Add ________________________

NOW TRY THIS!

7 000 000	800 000	50 000	4000	100	90	2

- Choose three cards and add them to make a number.

Example: 50 190 *(fifty thousand, one hundred and ninety)*

- Reverse the digits and find the difference.

$$\begin{array}{r} 50190 \\ -\ 09105 \\ \hline \end{array}$$

- Repeat for six different numbers.

Clue for questions 3 and 4: remember that subtraction is the inverse (opposite) of addition. If you know the answer to an addition question and one of the other numbers, you can use subtraction to find the missing number.

Understand and use decimal notation and place value

Figure it out!

1. With a partner, take turns to read aloud each number in the grid.
2. On the first line, write the value of the underlined digit in each number.
3. On the second line, write the value of the digit 3 in each number.

! Write each value in words and in figures.

	M	HTh	TTh	Th	H	T	U	t	h	th
(a)			8	3	2	1	1 •	0	$\underline{5}$	
(b)				5	7	$\underline{4}$	3 •			
(c)		$\underline{2}$	3	0	6	9	2 •	4		
(d)					3	9	8 •	2	8	$\underline{1}$
(e)		3	0	$\underline{9}$	0	4	8 •	7	5	
(f)	$\underline{5}$	7	1	1	8	2	7 •	3	6	9
(g)							0 •	$\underline{2}$	0	3

(a) *five-hundredths* $\frac{5}{100}$
three thousand 3000

(b) ______________________
____

(c) ______________________
____

(d) ______________________
____

(e) ______________________
____

(f) ______________________
____

(g) ______________________
____

B Complete these number patterns.

(a) Add 0.1 — 3.6, *3.7*, ___, ___, ___, ___, ___

(b) Add 0.01 — 4.05, ___, ___, ___, ___, ___, ___

(c) Subtract 0.1 — 8.3, ___, ___, ___, ___, ___, ___

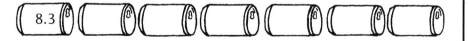

(d) Subtract 0.01 — 0.32, ___, ___, ___, ___, ___, ___

(e) Add ______ — 5.67, 5.78, ___, ___, ___, ___, ___

(f) Subtract ______ — 9.32, 9.23, ___, ___, ___, ___, ___

It is important to know what each digit in a number stands for. Make sure you know the column headings as shown in the table above. Digits to the right of the decimal point are worth less than one whole.

Figure it out!

Understand and use decimal notation and place value

C

1. Move along the track and write the difference between **adjacent** numbers.

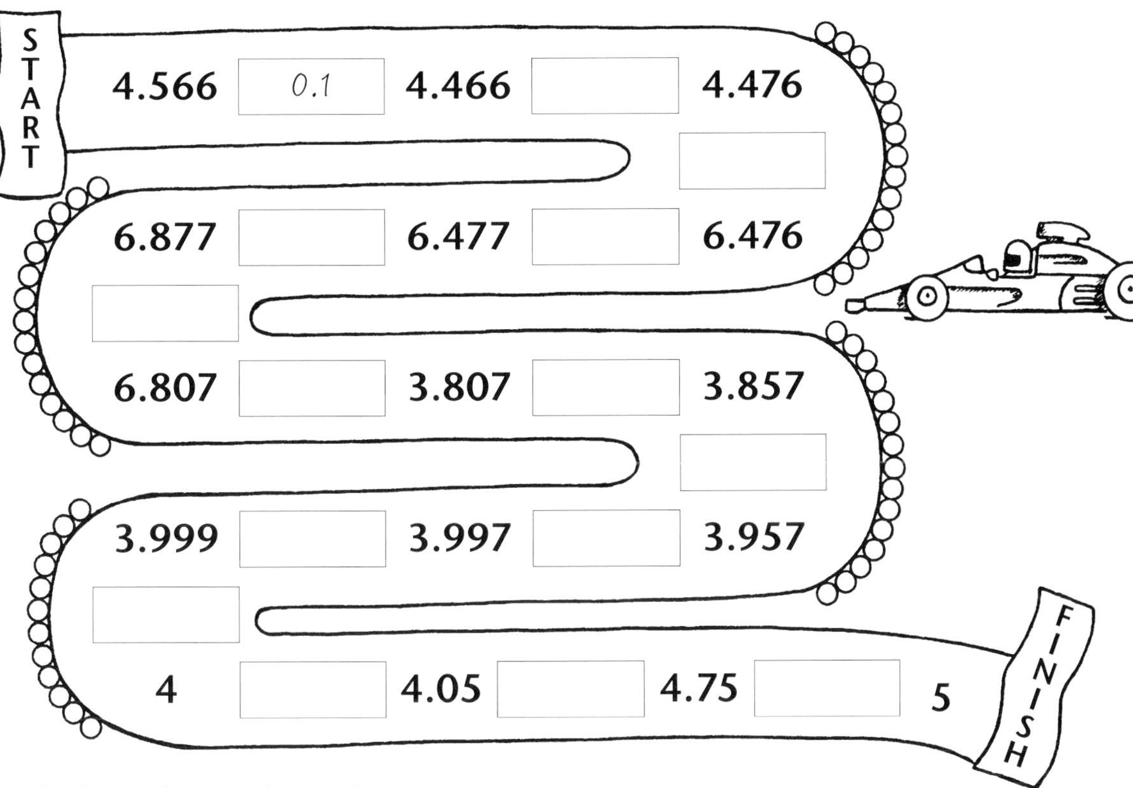

2. Which number on the track is:

(a) six point four seven six? 6.476 **(b)** six point eight zero seven?

(c) one-tenth more than 3.707? **(d)** one-tenth less than 4.666?

(e) one-hundredth less than 3.867? **(f)** one-hundredth more than 4.456?

(g) seven-thousandths more than 3.8?

3. Look at the differences you have written on the track. Which is:

(a) one-tenth? 0.1 **(b)** one-hundredth?

(c) one-thousandth? **(d)** four-hundredths?

(e) the largest? **(f)** the smallest?

NOW TRY THIS!

+0.001	+0.1	+0.01	+1

If you start with the number 4.683 and follow the cards in the order shown, you will get this number trail:

4.683, 4.684, 4.784, 4.794, 5.794

- With a partner, arrange the cards in different orders and write as many different number trails as you can. Each time, start with the number 4.683.

Adjacent means neighbouring. For the 'Now try this!' challenge, there are 24 different number trails to find.

Multiply/divide integers by 10, 100 or 1000

Move over!

A

1. Multiply these numbers by 10, 100 or 1000 by moving the digits to the left.

	M	HTh	TTh	Th	H	T	U	
(a)					5	7	4	× 10
				5	7	4	0	
(b)					8	2	9	× 100
(c)				2	0	5	0	× 1000
(d)				9	9	0	9	× 100

	M	HTh	TTh	Th	H	T	U	
(e)				4	0	5	8	× 100
(f)				6	8	0	0	× 1000
(g)			3	8	5	0	4	× 10
(h)				1	0	6	9	× 1000

2. Divide these numbers by 10, 100 or 1000 by moving the digits to the right.

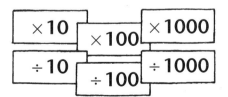

	M	HTh	TTh	Th	H	T	U	
(a)			4	2	0	3	0	÷ 10
				4	2	0	3	
(b)		1	2	7	0	0	0	÷ 100
(c)		6	0	8	0	0	0	÷ 1000
(d)	5	9	1	9	9	0	0	÷ 100

	M	HTh	TTh	Th	H	T	U	
(e)		2	0	5	8	0	0	÷ 100
(f)	9	1	4	4	0	0	0	÷ 1000
(g)	6	2	4	5	0	4	0	÷ 10
(h)	2	0	1	9	0	0	0	÷ 1000

B

Use the cards to complete the calculations.

× 10 **× 100** **× 1000** **÷ 10** **÷ 100** **÷ 1000**

(a) 493 [× 10] = 4930

(b) 49 300 [ ] = 493

(c) 4930 [ ] = 493 000

(d) 493 000 [ ] = 4930

(e) 493 [ ] = 493 000

(f) 4930 [ ] = 4 930 000

(g) 49 300 [ ] = 4930

(h) 493 000 [ ] = 49 300

When you multiply positive numbers by 10, 100 or 1000, the digits move to the **left** to make the number larger. When you divide positive numbers by 10, 100 or 1000, the digits move to the **right** to make the number smaller. Remember that multiplication is the inverse (opposite) of division, and vice versa.

Move over!

Multiply/divide integers by 10, 100 or 1000

C

1. A charity shop sells books at **one-tenth** of the original price.
Write the sale prices of these books in pounds and pence.

Original price	£10	£9	£5	£18	£12
Sale price	______	______	______	______	______

2. These people give part of their annual salary to charity.
Work out how much money each person gives and how much money each has left.

! To find one-tenth, or 'ten per cent', divide by 10.
To find one-hundredth, or 'one per cent', divide by 100.
To find one-thousandth, divide by 1000.

(a)

I earn £9920 per year and give one-tenth to charity.

Gives ______

Has left ______

(b)

I earn £32 300 per year and give one-hundredth to charity.

Gives ______

Has left ______

(c)

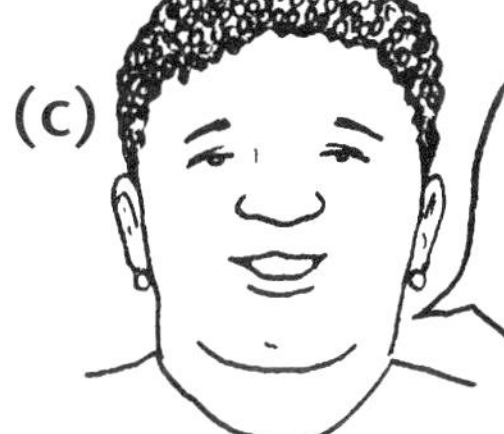

I earn £15 490 per year and give ten per cent to charity.

Gives ______

Has left ______

(d)

I earn £58 000 per year and give one-thousandth to charity.

Gives ______

Has left ______

(e)

I earn £11 600 per year and give one per cent to charity.

Gives ______

Has left ______

(f)

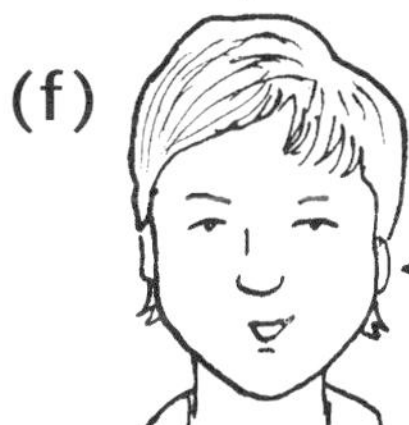

I earn £102 000 per year and give one-thousandth to charity.

Gives ______

Has left ______

NOW TRY THIS!

- Choose a number from the first grid and an instruction from the second. How many answers can you make between 0 and 3000?

245 600	34
5000	87 000
20	230

×1000	÷10
×100	÷100
×10	÷1000

Example:
20 x 10 = 200

If a whole number does not end in zeros, for example £4, be careful when you divide by 10, 100 or 1000. Remember to think of the digits moving to the right past the decimal point: £4 ÷ 10 = £0.40 or 40 p; £4 ÷ 100 = £0.04 or 4 p.

Multiply/divide integers and decimals by 10, 100 or 1000

Decimal digits

A

1. Multiply these numbers by 10, 100 or 1000 by moving the digits to the left.

	TTh	Th	H	T	U	t	h	
(a)					3	8		× 10
				3	8			
(b)					4	1		× 100
(c)				4	3	9	7	× 1000
(d)				8	6	0	9	× 100

	TTh	Th	H	T	U	t	h	
(e)				2	0	2	3	× 10
(f)				8	2	1		× 1000
(g)			7	6	2	0	6	× 10
(h)				1	0	4	5	× 1000

2. Divide these numbers by 10, 100 or 1000 by moving the digits to the right.

	TTh	Th	H	T	U	t	h	
(a)				5	7			÷ 10
					5	7		
(b)			8	2	2			÷ 100
(c)		5	0	6	0			÷ 1000
(d)		1	9	4	5	2		÷ 10

	TTh	Th	H	T	U	t	h	
(e)			3	0	5	8		÷ 10
(f)			5	4	0			÷ 100
(g)		4	1	1	0	4		÷ 10
(h)	2	0	2	9	0			÷ 1000

B

Fill in the answers to complete the patterns.

3670	× 1000	= 3 670 000	2450	× 1000	= 2 450 000
3670	× 100	=	2450	× 100	=
3670	× 10	=	2450	× 10	=
3670	× 1	=	2450	× 1	=
3670	÷ 10	=	2450	÷ 10	=
3670	÷ 100	= 36.7	2450	÷ 100	=
3670	÷ 1000	=	2450	÷ 1000	=

When you multiply positive numbers by 10, 100 or 1000, the digits move to the **left** to make the number larger. When you divide positive numbers by 10, 100 or 1000, the digits move to the **right** to make the number smaller. Remember that the decimal point does not move!

Decimal digits

Multiply/divide integers and decimals by 10, 100 or 1000

C

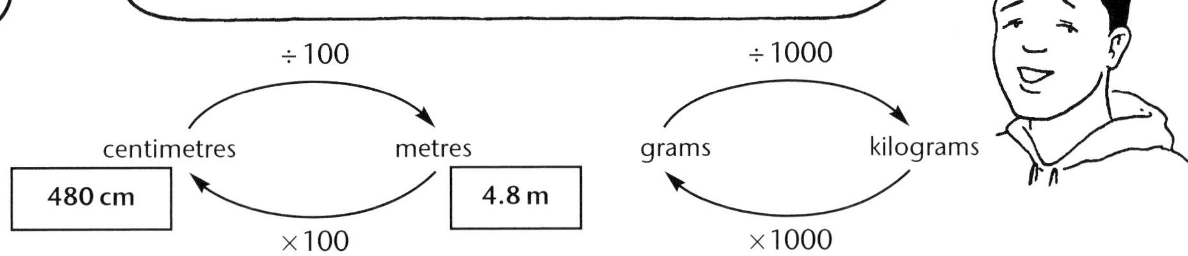

1. Convert these measurements by multiplying or dividing by 100 or 1000.

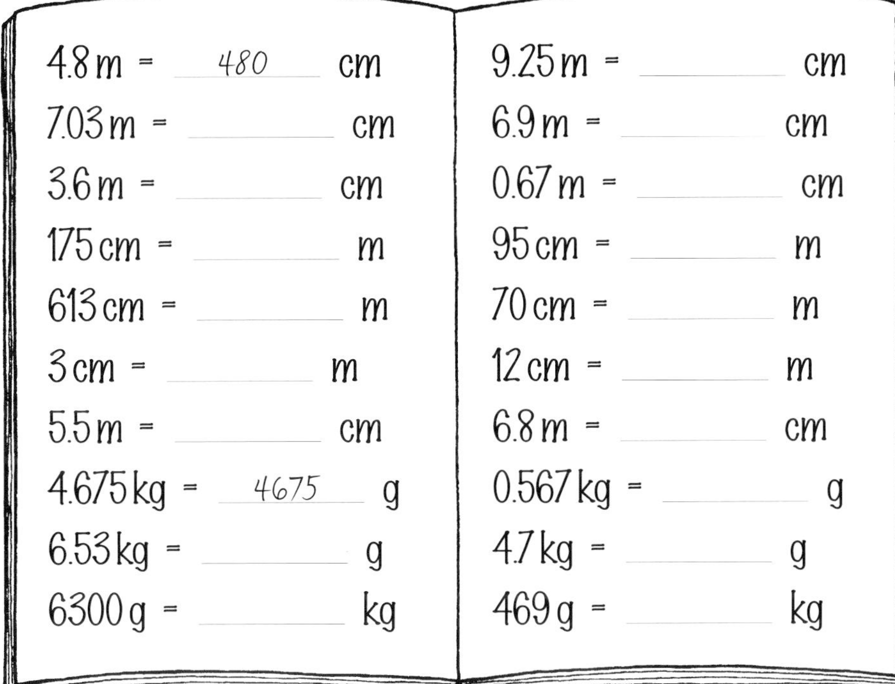

4.8 m = 480 cm
7.03 m = ______ cm
3.6 m = ______ cm
175 cm = ______ m
613 cm = ______ m
3 cm = ______ m
5.5 m = ______ cm
4.675 kg = 4675 g
6.53 kg = ______ g
6300 g = ______ kg
9.25 m = ______ cm
6.9 m = ______ cm
0.67 m = ______ cm
95 cm = ______ m
70 cm = ______ m
12 cm = ______ m
6.8 m = ______ cm
0.567 kg = ______ g
4.7 kg = ______ g
469 g = ______ kg

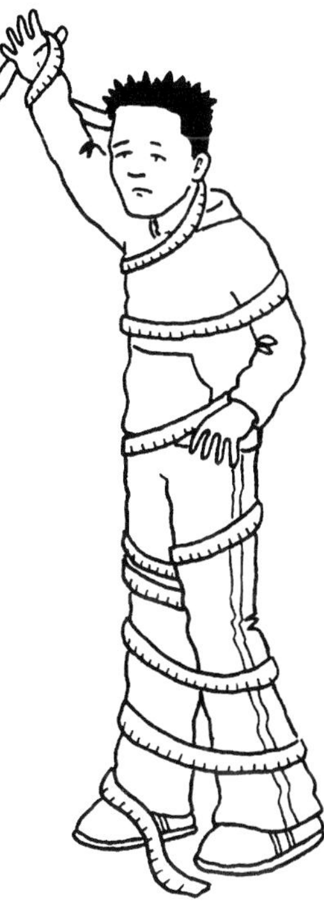

2. What would you multiply by to convert 5 cm to millimetres? ______

NOW TRY THIS!

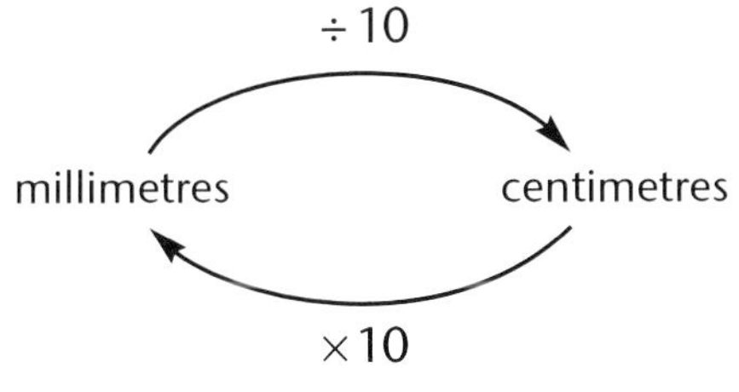

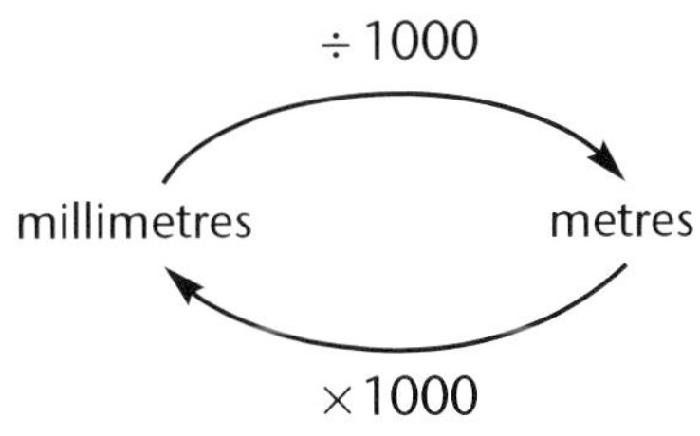

- Use these cards to make at least 15 pairs of equal measurements. You do not have to use all the cards each time.

6	6	0	0	0	0	4	4	.	.	m	cm	mm

Example: 6 . 4 m = 6 4 0 cm

When you multiply positive numbers by 10, 100 or 1000, the digits move to the **left** to make the number larger. When you divide positive numbers by 10, 100 or 1000, the digits move to the **right** to make the number smaller. Remember that the decimal point does not move!

Compare and order decimals, including units of measurement

Correct order of play?

Write the decimals in the correct boxes on the number lines.

(a)

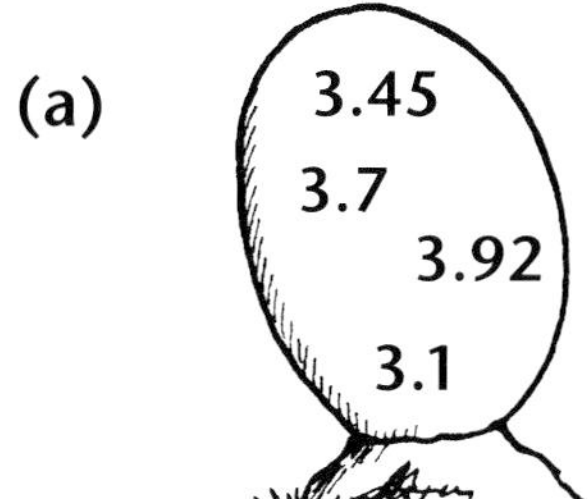

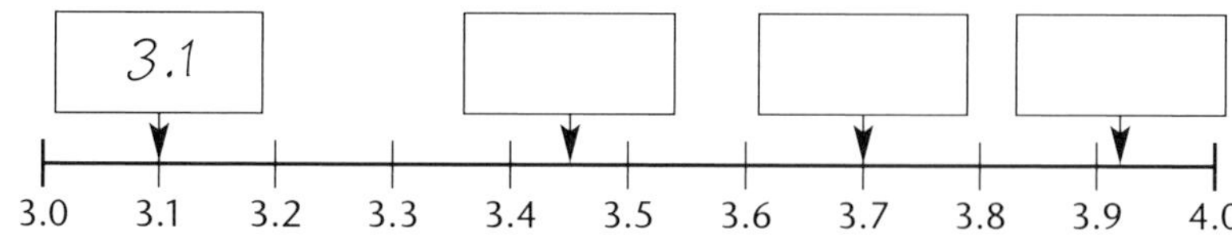

(b)

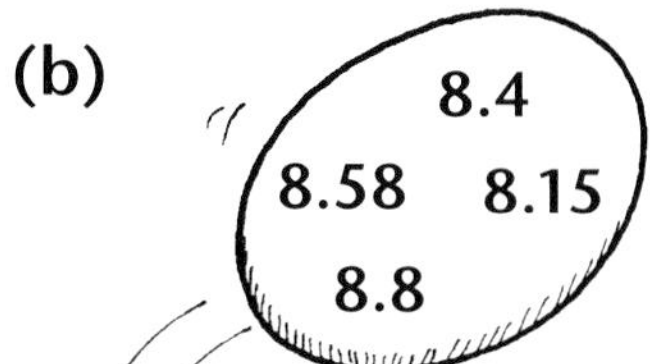

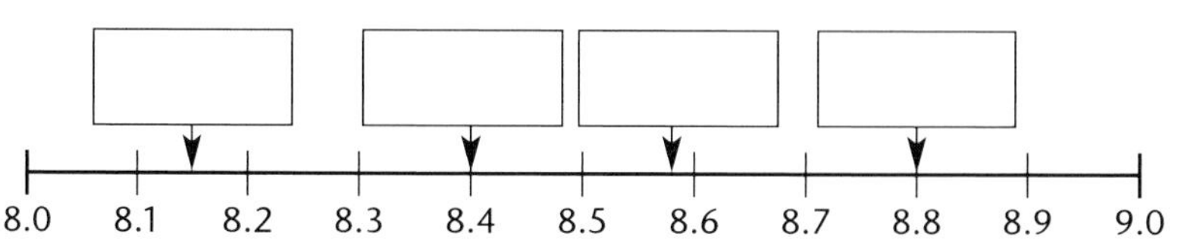

(c)

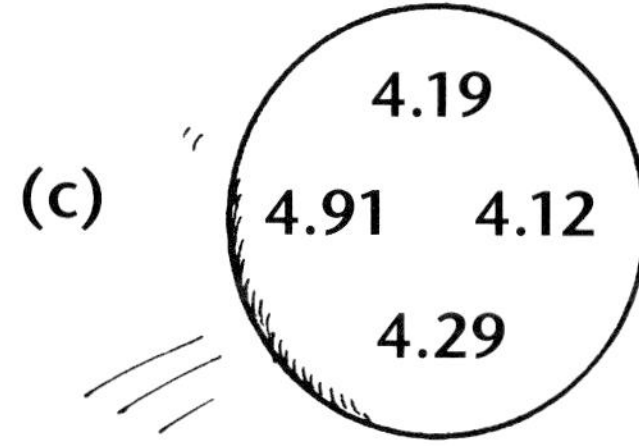

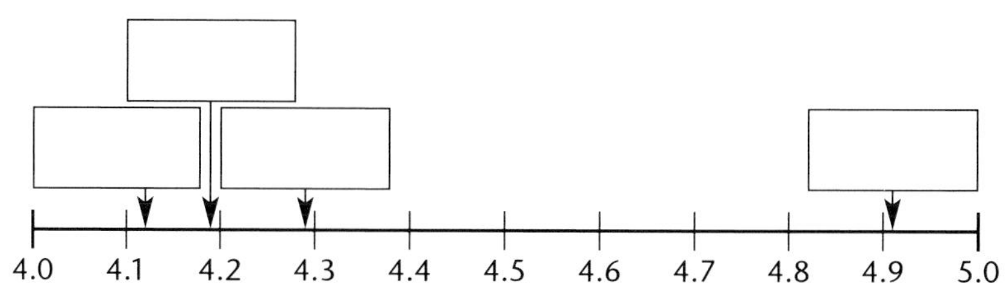

(d)

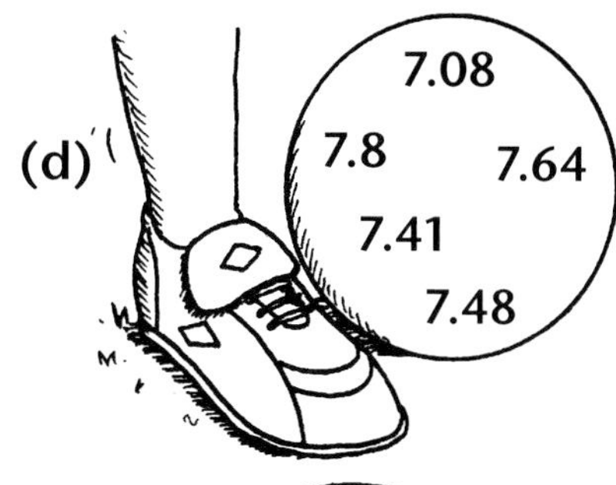

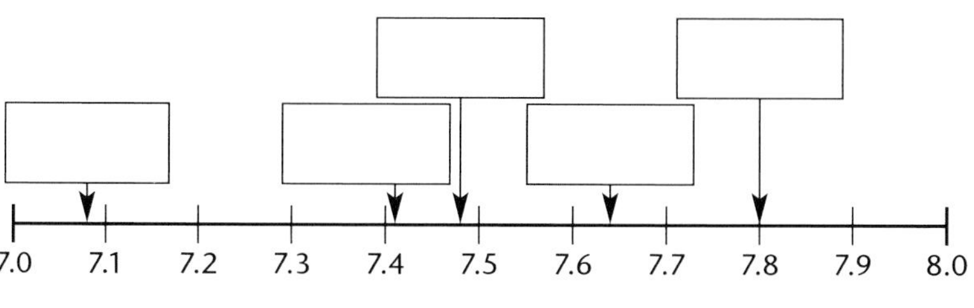

(e)

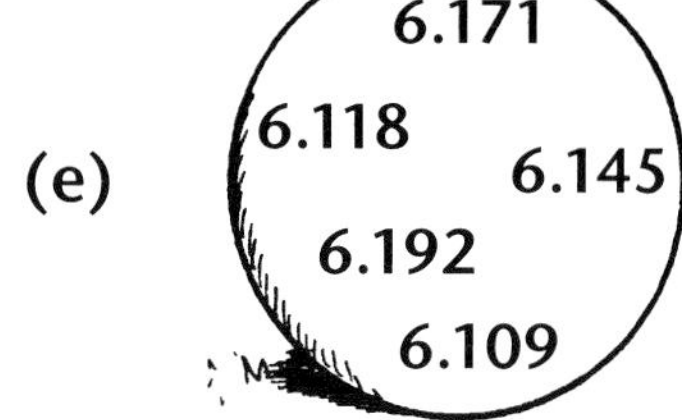

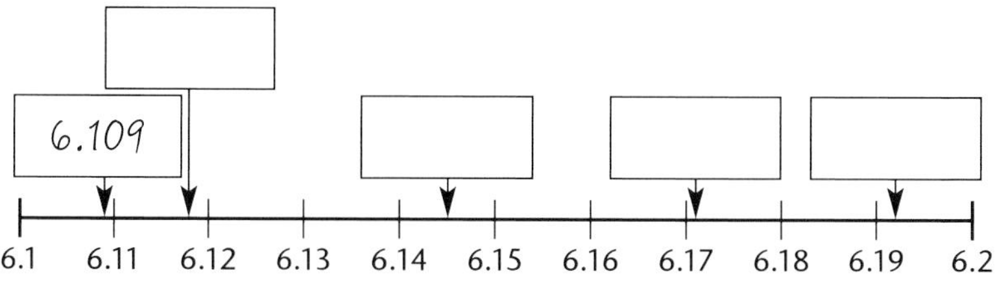

Arrange the measurements in each group in ascending order.

(a)	0.31 m	2.4 m	2.13 m	2.04 m	0.31 m,
(b)	6.06 l	0.6 l	6.6 l	0.66 l	
(c)	5.31 km	5.4 km	5.13 km	5.04 km	
(d)	1.892 kg	1.982 kg	1.829 kg	1.9 kg	
(e)	0.018 m	0.08 m	0.1 m	0.081 m	

When you are comparing and ordering decimals it is sometimes helpful to write the decimals in columns, lining up the decimal points. Then compare the digits in each column, starting with the column furthest to the left. **Ascending order** means in order from smallest to largest.

Correct order of play?

Compare and order decimals, including units of measurement

C

1. These are measurements of playing areas and ball sizes for three sports.

	Playing area		
Sport	**length**	**width**	**Ball diameter**
Football	0.12 km	90 m	22.2 cm
Lacrosse	100 m	0.064 km	65 mm
Volleyball	0.018 km	0.009 km	21.3 cm

Which sport has: **(a)** the longest playing area length? __________

(b) the narrowest playing area width? __________ **(c)** the smallest ball diameter? __________

2. These are the lengths of some playing areas. Write the lengths in **ascending order**.

Football	**Lacrosse**	**Volleyball**	**Hockey**
0.12 km	100 m	0.018 km	91.4 m

____

3. These are measurements of playing areas and ball sizes for other sports.

	Playing area		
Sport	**length**	**width**	**Ball diameter**
Hockey	91.4 m	54.9 m	73 mm
Snooker	3.66 m	187 cm	5.2 cm
Squash	875 cm	6.4 m	4.15 cm
Tennis (singles)	23.77 m	8.23 m	6.67 cm
Table tennis	274 cm	156 cm	38 mm

Which of these five sports has: **(a)** the shortest playing area length? __________

(b) the widest playing area width? __________ **(c)** the smallest ball diameter? __________

4. Convert all the ball diameters on the sheet to centimetres. Write them in descending order.

22.2 cm, __________

NOW TRY THIS!

- Rearrange these cards to make 20 different decimals.

  2 | . | 4 | 0 | 6

- Arrange the decimals to make 10 true statements using the greater than (>) and less than (<) signs.

  Examples: 4.206 > 4.062
  4.062 < 4.206

Remember that 1000 m equals 1 km, so to convert a measurement in metres to kilometres you divide by 1000. There are 10 mm in 1 cm, so to convert from millimetres to centimetres you divide by 10. **Ascending order** means in order from smallest to largest. **Descending order** means in order from largest to smallest.

Round positive whole numbers to the nearest 10, 100, 1000

Round and round

Contestants on a gameshow are dealt digit cards to make large money prizes.

(a) Arrange each contestant's digits to make the largest number possible.

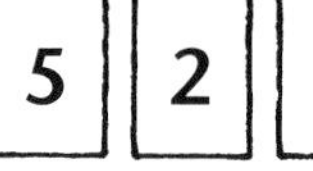

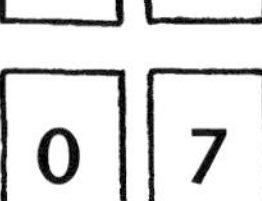

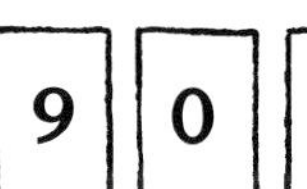

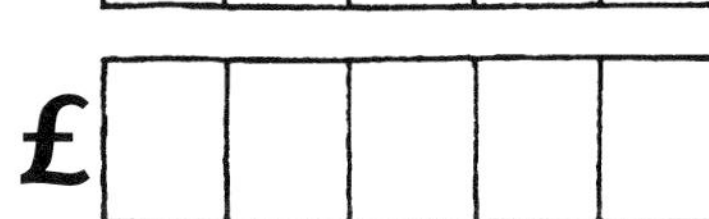

Contestant						
Julie	~~5~~	~~1~~	7	4	9	£ _ _ 5 _ 1
Ahmed	6	2	1	7	1	£
Paula	3	8	5	2	8	£
Clive	4	9	2	2	6	£
Nicole	6	5	9	2	5	£
David	0	7	9	0	8	£

(b) Write all the numbers in **descending order**.

98 700, ____________________

(c) Complete this table by rounding each number to the nearest 10, 100 and 1000.

Go back to the original number each time before rounding. **!**

Number	To nearest 10	To nearest 100	To nearest 1000
98 700			

B

1. Round each number to the nearest 1000 and join it with a line.

98 529   97 489   99 501   99 499   99 517   100 741

97 000   98 000   99 000   100 000   101 000

98 699   98 480   96 500   97 541   100 388   99 801

2. What are the lowest and highest possible integers that round to 98 000?

Lowest ____________ Highest ____________

Descending order means in order from largest to smallest. When you round to the nearest 10 the answer will be a multiple of 10, when you round to the nearest 100 the answer will be a multiple of 100, and when you round to the nearest 1000 the answer will be a multiple of 1000. Remember that an integer is a positive or negative whole number.

Round and round

Round positive whole numbers to the nearest 10, 100, 1000

1. Write the probabilities in these newspaper reports more appropriately by rounding the numbers. State what you have rounded the number to.

a The probability of snow falling on Christmas Day in London this year has been predicted as one in **22**.

20 (to nearest 10)

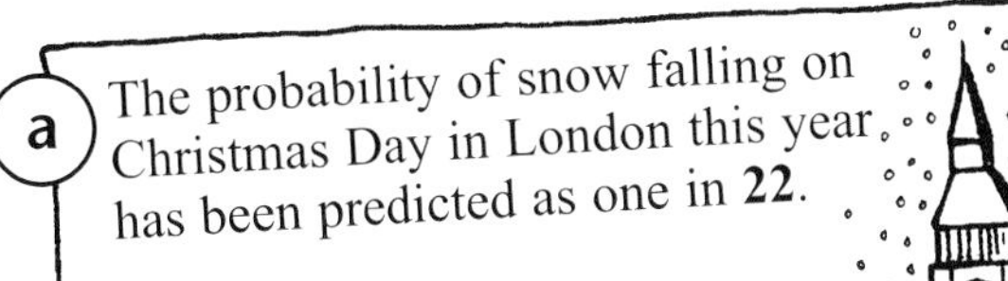

b The chance of a mother having triplets is one in **6794**.

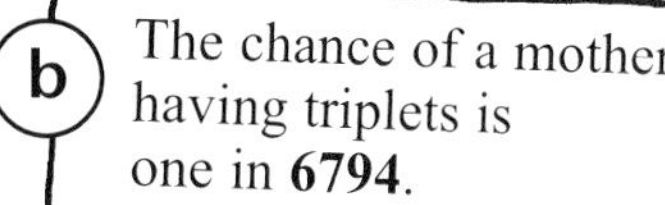

c The chance in Australia of being eaten by a shark is one in **1 681 818**.

d The probability of rolling four sixes one after another with a fair dice is one in **1296**.

e The probability of picking the King and Queen of Hearts one after another from a pack of cards is one in **2652**.

f The chance of having an allergy to peanuts is one in **178**.

g The chance of being struck by lightning is one in **709 260**.

h The probability of guessing a person's four-letter password is one in **456 976**.

i The probability of picking the Ace, King, Queen and Jack of Spades one after another from a pack of cards is one in **6 497 400**.

j The chance of winning the Lottery is one in every **13 983 816**.

2. Work out approximate answers to these questions, by rounding.

(a) $496 \times 11 \approx$ 500 x 10 = 5000 **(b)** $8102 \times 49 \approx$

(c) $395 \times 902 \approx$ **(d)** $726 \times 792 \approx$

NOW TRY THIS!

- Write ten whole numbers that Jo could be thinking of.

I'm thinking of a number that when rounded to the nearest 100 is 47 000...
...and when rounded to the nearest 10 is 47 000.

Newspapers often have rounded numbers in their reports. Rounding is very useful when calculating, as it can help you to find an approximate answer. In C1 you might have different answers from someone else.

Round decimals to the nearest whole number or tenth

Round pounds

Round each amount of money to the nearest pound and to the nearest ten pence.

(a)

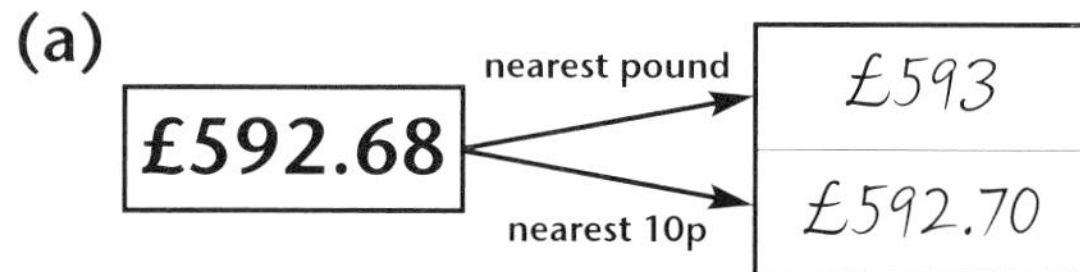

(b)

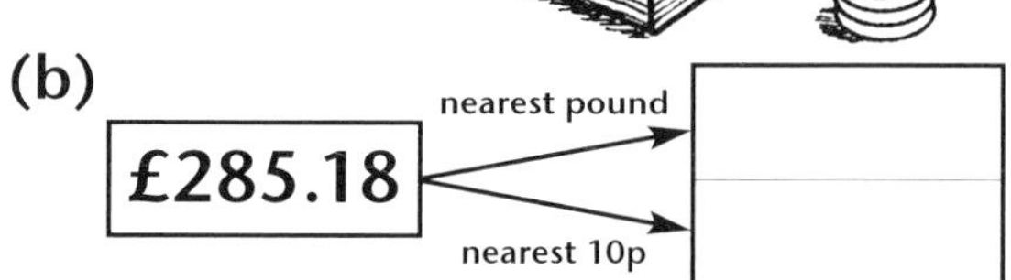

(c)

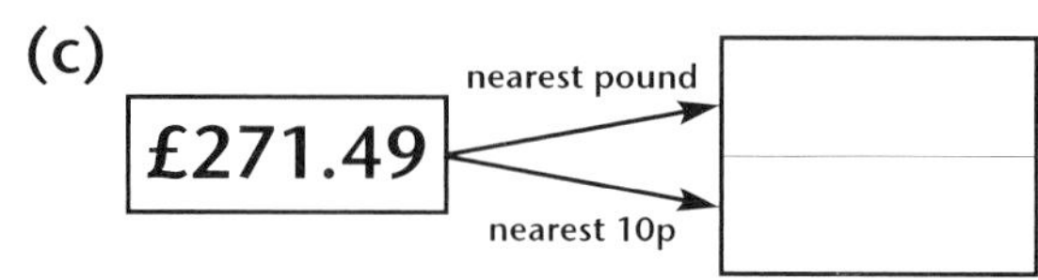

(d)

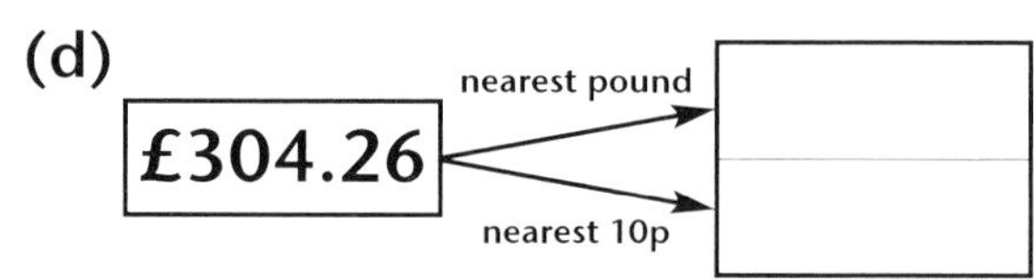

(e)

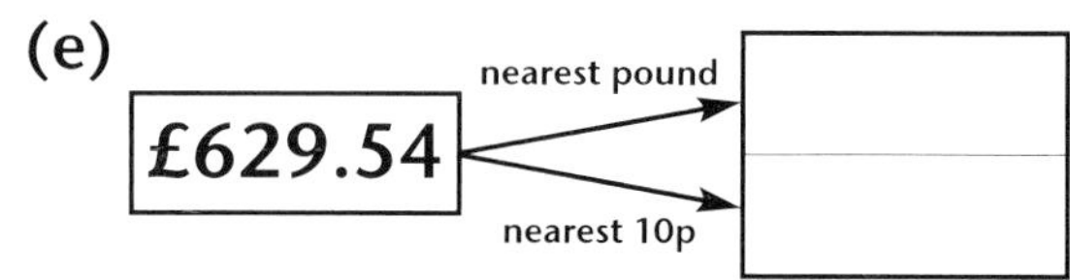

(f)

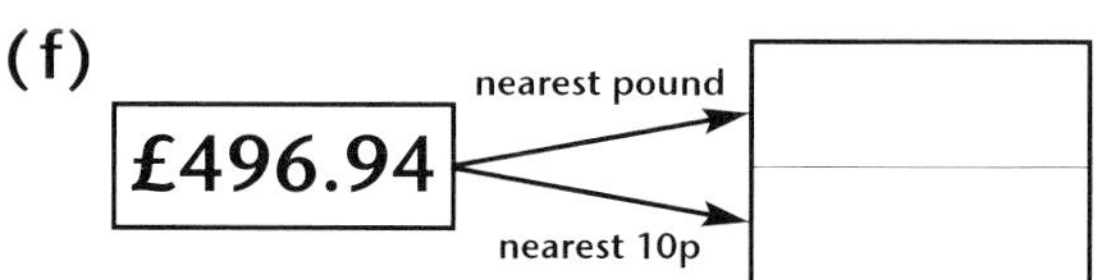

(g)

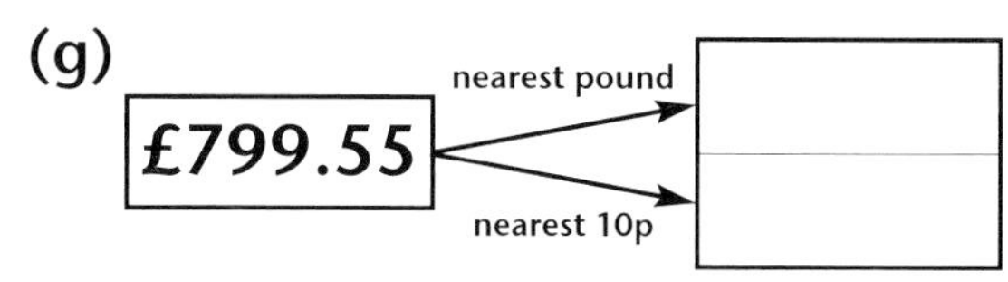

(h)

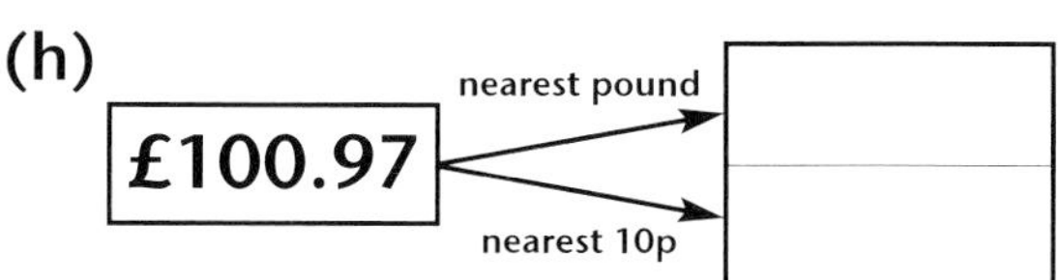

B

Pick two numbers from below and divide the larger by the smaller. Round the answer to the nearest whole number and to the nearest tenth (one decimal place).

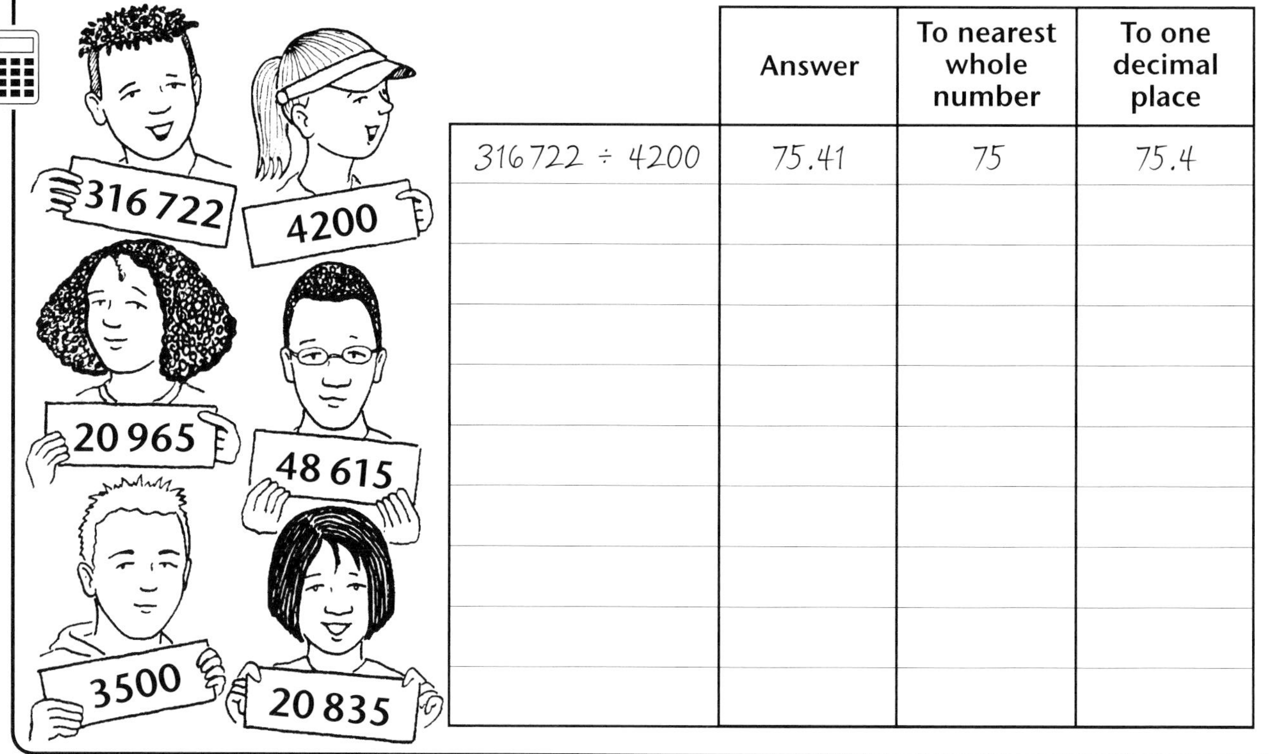

	Answer	To nearest whole number	To one decimal place
316722 ÷ 4200	75.41	75	75.4

Rounding to the nearest tenth is also called rounding to one decimal place. This is where the answers will have one digit after the decimal point, for example 5.8, 13.4, 6.0. Notice that you write 6.0 rather than 6, to show that the answer is rounded to one decimal place.

Round pounds

Round decimals to the nearest whole number or tenth

C

1. Use a calculator to do these divisions. Round the answer shown on the display to give a sensible answer. Think carefully about whether to round up or down for each situation.

(a) Lauren wants to buy as many 26p stamps as she can. How many can she buy with £7.57?

Calculator: 29.115384

Sensible answer: 29

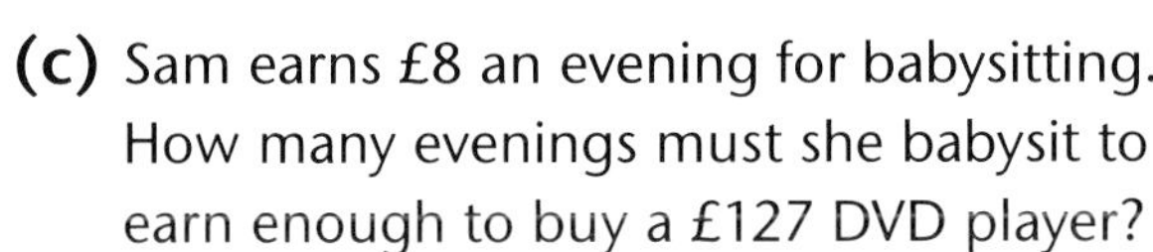

(b) Mum saves £36 per week. In how many weeks will she save enough to buy a £394 washing machine?

Calculator: ____________

Sensible answer: ____________

(c) Sam earns £8 an evening for babysitting. How many evenings must she babysit to earn enough to buy a £127 DVD player?

Calculator: ____________

Sensible answer: ____________

(d) Pete has £23.47. He wants to buy as many £1.49 pens as he can. How many can he buy?

Calculator: ____________

Sensible answer: ____________

(e) Alia has 247 two pence coins. She puts them into moneybags that hold exactly 50 two pence coins. How many moneybags does she need?

Calculator: ____________

Sensible answer: ____________

(f) Mr Gray has 143 twenty pence coins. He gives each of his three children the same number of coins. What is the maximum number each child can get?

Calculator: ____________

Sensible answer: ____________

(g) 13 people share the Lottery jackpot of £574 427. How much does each person get?

Calculator: ____________

Sensible answer: ____________

(h) The cost of Ahmed's phone calls is £17.50. He made 13 calls. What is the average cost of each call?

Calculator: ____________

Sensible answer: ____________

2. Work out approximate answers to these questions, by rounding.

(a) $29.78 \times 5.8 \approx$ $30 \times 6 = 180$

(b) $1.48 \times 19.95 \approx$ ____________

(c) $24.7 \times 3.91 \approx$ ____________

(d) $10.18 \times 7.89 \approx$ ____________

NOW TRY THIS!

- Write nine decimals that Dec could be thinking of.

I'm thinking of a decimal that has two digits after the decimal point...
...when rounded to the nearest **whole number** it is 9...
...and when rounded to the nearest **tenth** it is 8.7.

When you are answering division questions, think carefully about the situation. Sometimes a number like 5.78 is rounded **down** because 5 is a more sensible answer than 5.8 or 6 (for example, how many people can fit in a car). In C2 you may have different answers from someone else. Talk to a partner about why this might be.

Understand and order positive and negative integers

Are you positive?

A Join these positive and negative numbers to the correct places on the number lines.

(a)

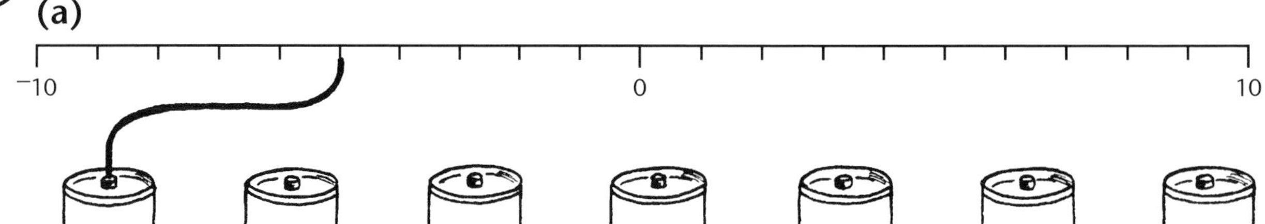

(b)

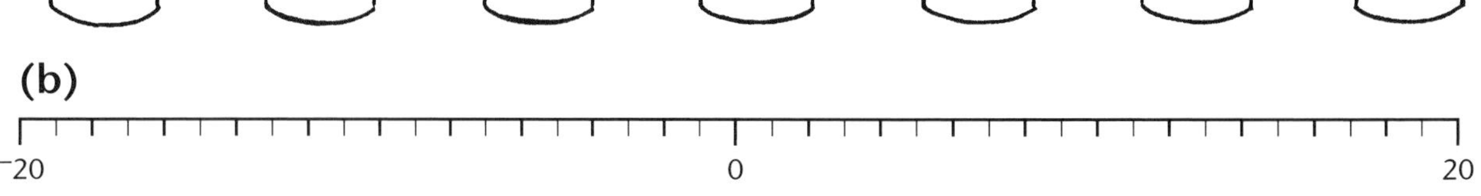

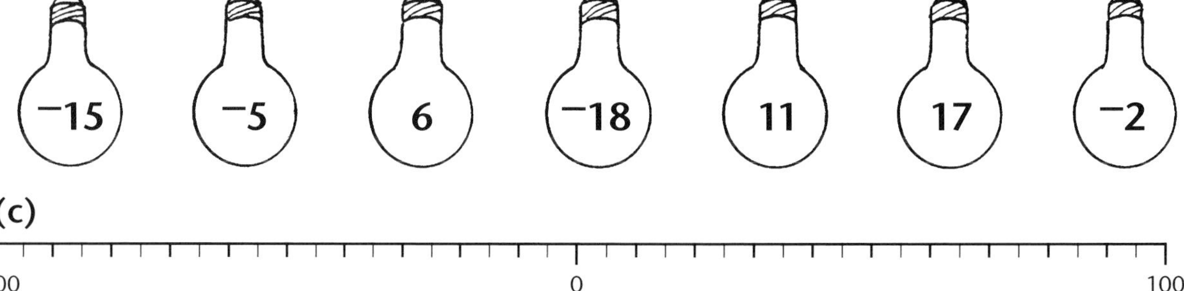

(c)

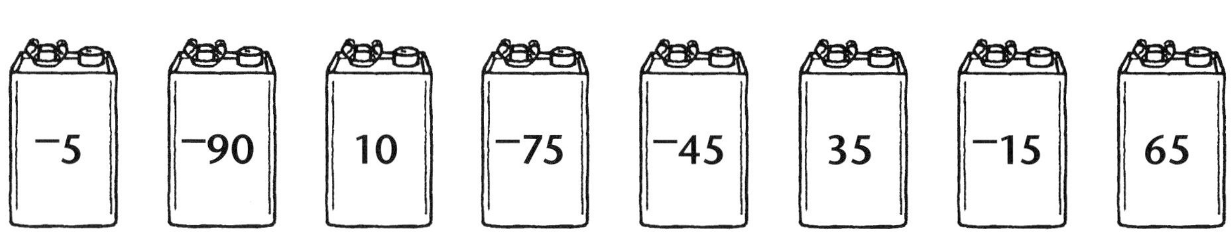

B

1. Fill in the < or > sign.

(a) ⁻6	<	⁻2	**(b)** ⁻5		⁻6	**(c)** ⁻9		⁻11
(d) ⁻22		⁻17	**(e)** ⁻21		⁻20	**(f)** ⁻14		⁻18
(g) ⁻45		⁻53	**(h)** ⁻37		⁻40	**(i)** ⁻55		⁻41
(j) ⁻73		⁻74	**(k)** ⁻78		⁻87	**(l)** ⁻91		⁻89
(m) ⁻99		1	**(n)** ⁻174		⁻108	**(o)** ⁻494		⁻748

2. Arrange the numbers in each group in **ascending order**.

(a) ⁻44 12 ⁻38 ⁻47 33 ⁻47, ____________

(b) ⁻472 ⁻268 178 ⁻297 26 ____________

(c) ⁻921 ⁻27 538 ⁻538 921 ____________

Remember that negative numbers work in a different way from positive numbers. With positive numbers 5 is larger than 4, but with negative numbers ⁻5 is **smaller** than ⁻4. **Ascending order** means in order from smallest to largest.

Are you positive?

Understand and order positive and negative integers

Palaeontologists have drawn a map to show exactly where they found some bones and fossils.

1. Label the *x*-axis and the *y*-axis of this grid with the **integers** from $^{-}8$ to 8.

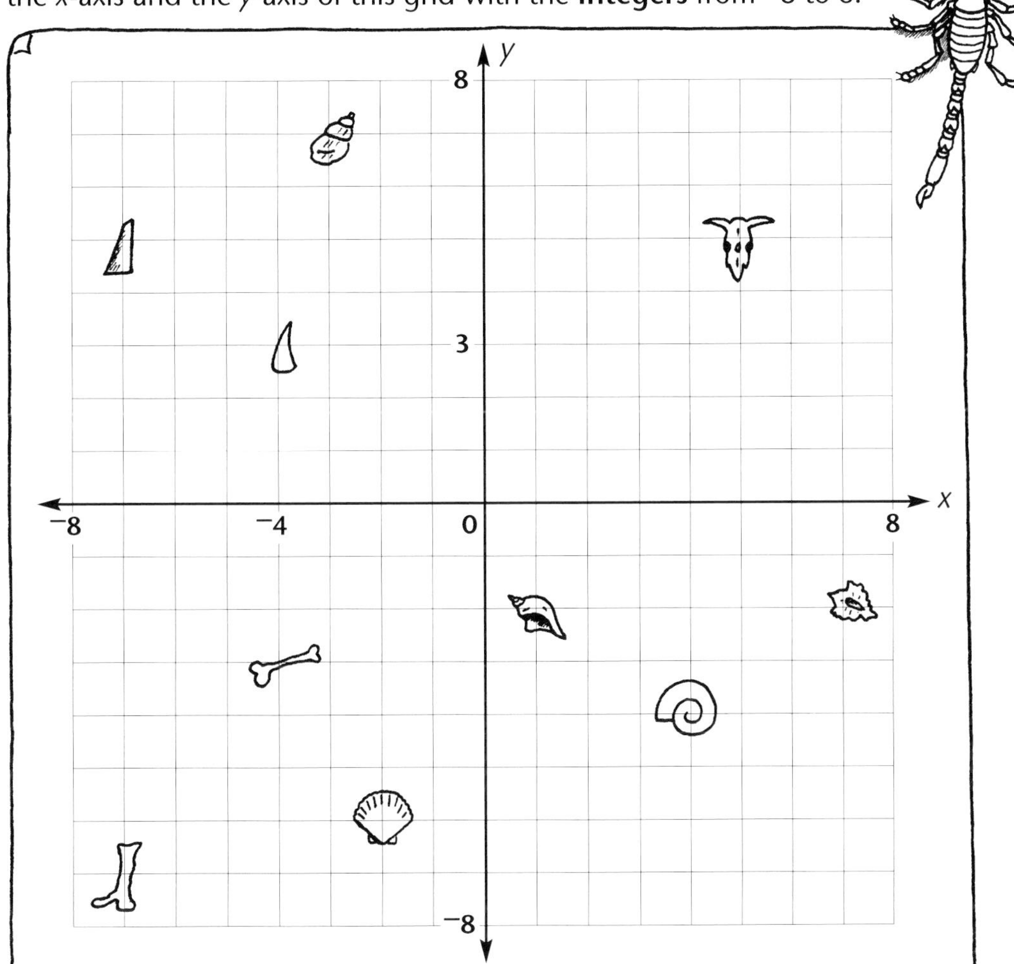

2. A shark's tooth was found at ($^{-}4$,3).
Write the coordinates of these bones and fossils.

Remember to write the **x** *coordinate before the* **y** *coordinate.*

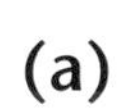   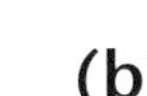    

(a) (___ , ___) (b) (___ , ___) (c) (___ , ___)

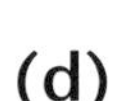   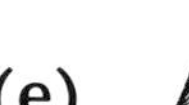   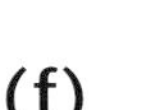 

(d) (___ , ___) (e) (___ , ___) (f) (___ , ___)

(g) (___ , ___) (h) (___ , ___) (i) (___ , ___)

NOW TRY THIS!

- Arrange these cards to make 12 different negative integers. Use as many of the digit cards as you wish.

−	3	3	3	4	5

- Arrange the negative integers to make ten true statements using the > and < signs.

Example: $^{-}33 > {}^{-}354$

$^{-}354 < {}^{-}33$

An **integer** is a whole number and can be positive, negative or zero, for example $^{-}12$, 6, 0, $^{-}54$, 16. Decimals and fractions are not integers as they are not whole numbers.

Add and subtract positive and negative integers

Up and down

1. Follow the lift's movements, starting at the ground floor (zero). Write which floor the lift stops at each time.

2. Write each instruction as an addition or subtraction statement. Use + for up and use – for down.

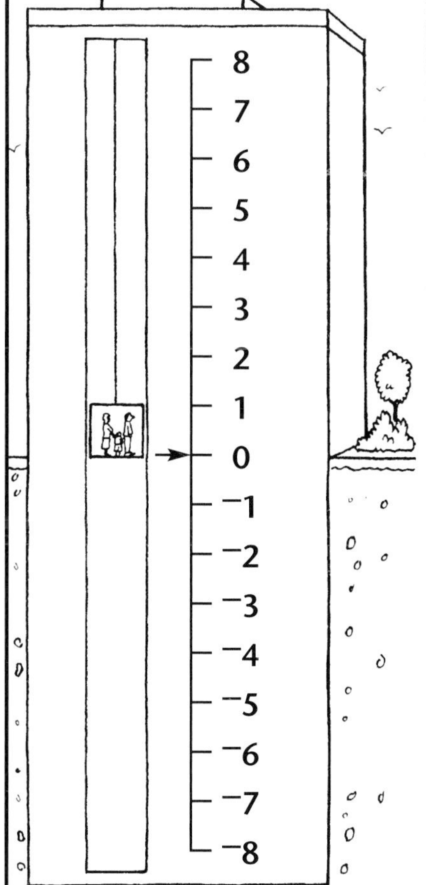

From floor		To floor	
0	down 6	−6	0 − 6 = −6
−6	up 8		
	down 4		
	up 9		
	down 7		
	down 5		
	up 8		
	down 6		
	down 2		
	up 4		
	down 6		
	up 11		
	down 7		
	down 2		
	up 7		

B In a quiz, contestants score 2 points for a correct answer, –3 points for an incorrect answer and –1 point for a pass. What does each contestant score in total?

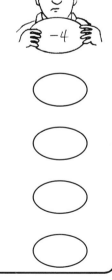

								Total
(a)	correct	incorrect	correct	incorrect	correct	pass	incorrect	
	2	−3	2	−3	2	−1	−3	−4
(b)	correct	correct	pass	incorrect	incorrect	incorrect	correct	
(c)	pass	incorrect	correct	incorrect	correct	pass	correct	
(d)	pass	correct	correct	incorrect	incorrect	correct	pass	
(e)	incorrect	incorrect	incorrect	correct	correct	pass	correct	

Counting up or down the number line will help you. It is sometimes useful to use zero as a 'stopover' when adding or subtracting: for example, if you are answering 6 – 9 = ?, go down from 6 to zero first, and then down three more to find the answer (⁻3).

Up and down

Add and subtract positive and negative integers

C

Sometimes an addition or subtraction sign appears next to a negative sign.

1.

I owe Sarah some money. My debt is £4, so I have ⁻4. I want to take away this debt, so I give Sarah her money back.
My debt **take away** my debt
$^{-}4 - {}^{-}4 = {}^{-}4 + 4 = 0$

Answer these questions. Rewrite them to help you.

(a) $5 - {}^{-}4 =$ 9

5 + 4 = 9

(b) $^{-}7 - {}^{-}8 =$ ☐

(c) $2 - {}^{-}5 =$ ☐

(d) $^{-}9 - {}^{-}5 =$ ☐

(e) $6 - {}^{-}3 =$ ☐

(f) $^{-}5 - {}^{-}6 =$ ☐

(g) $4 - {}^{-}7 =$ ☐

(h) $^{-}6 - {}^{-}6 =$ ☐

(i) $^{-}10 - {}^{-}8 =$ ☐

(j) $13 - {}^{-}8 =$ ☐

(k) $^{-}18 - {}^{-}11 =$ ☐

(l) $^{-}21 - {}^{-}16 =$ ☐

2.

I have a debt of £10, so my balance is ⁻10. I add another £3 of debt to this.
My debt **plus** more debt
$^{-}10 + {}^{-}3 = {}^{-}10 - 3 = {}^{-}13$

Answer these questions. Rewrite them to help you.

(a) $5 + {}^{-}4 =$ 1

5 − 4 = 1

(b) $^{-}7 + {}^{-}2 =$ ☐

(c) $4 + {}^{-}6 =$ ☐

(d) $^{-}3 + {}^{-}4 =$ ☐

(e) $8 + {}^{-}3 =$ ☐

(f) $^{-}4 + {}^{-}6 =$ ☐

(g) $^{-}3 + {}^{-}7 =$ ☐

(h) $^{-}6 + {}^{-}6 =$ ☐

(i) $10 + {}^{-}8 =$ ☐

(j) $^{-}9 + {}^{-}8 =$ ☐

(k) $^{-}12 + {}^{-}8 =$ ☐

(l) $21 + {}^{-}27 =$ ☐

NOW TRY THIS!

- Complete these magic squares so that each row, column and diagonal has the total shown.

Total 3

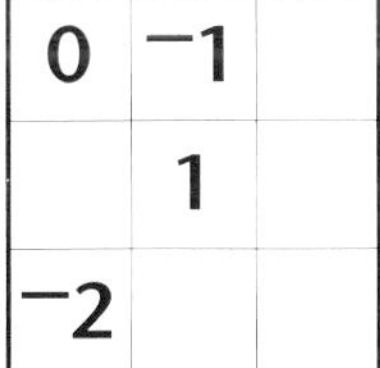

0	$^{-}1$	
	1	
$^{-}2$		

Total −3

		2
3		
$^{-}4$		0

Total −9

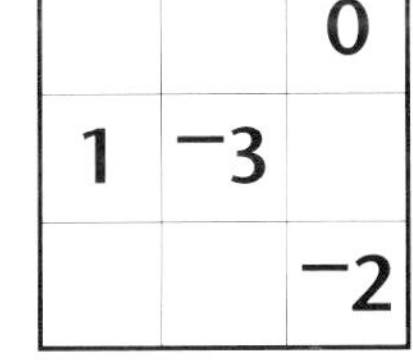

		0
1	$^{-}3$	
		$^{-}2$

Think of subtracting a negative as 'plus' and think of adding a negative as 'subtract'. The squares are 'magic' because each row, column and diagonal has the same total. In the first magic square, each row, column and diagonal has a total of 3.

Recognise and use multiples and primes

Special numbers

A

1. Write the first 12 multiples of 3, 4, 5, 6, 7, 8 and 9.

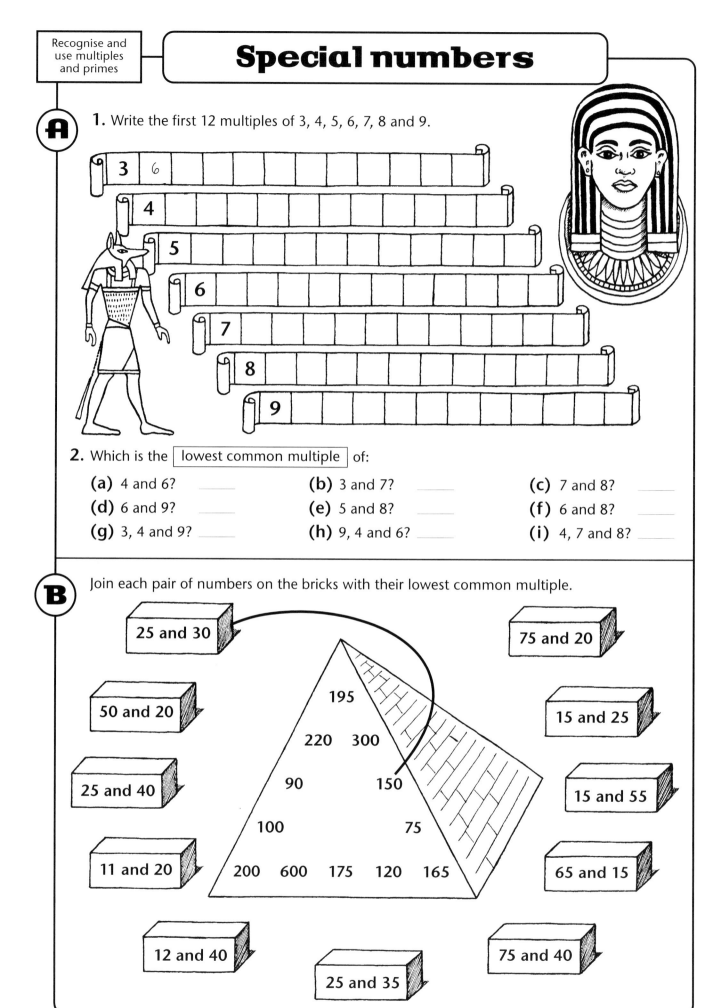

3	6										
4											
5											
6											
7											
8											
9											

2. Which is the lowest common multiple of:

(a) 4 and 6? ____ **(b)** 3 and 7? ____ **(c)** 7 and 8? ____

(d) 6 and 9? ____ **(e)** 5 and 8? ____ **(f)** 6 and 8? ____

(g) 3, 4 and 9? ____ **(h)** 9, 4 and 6? ____ **(i)** 4, 7 and 8? ____

B

Join each pair of numbers on the bricks with their lowest common multiple.

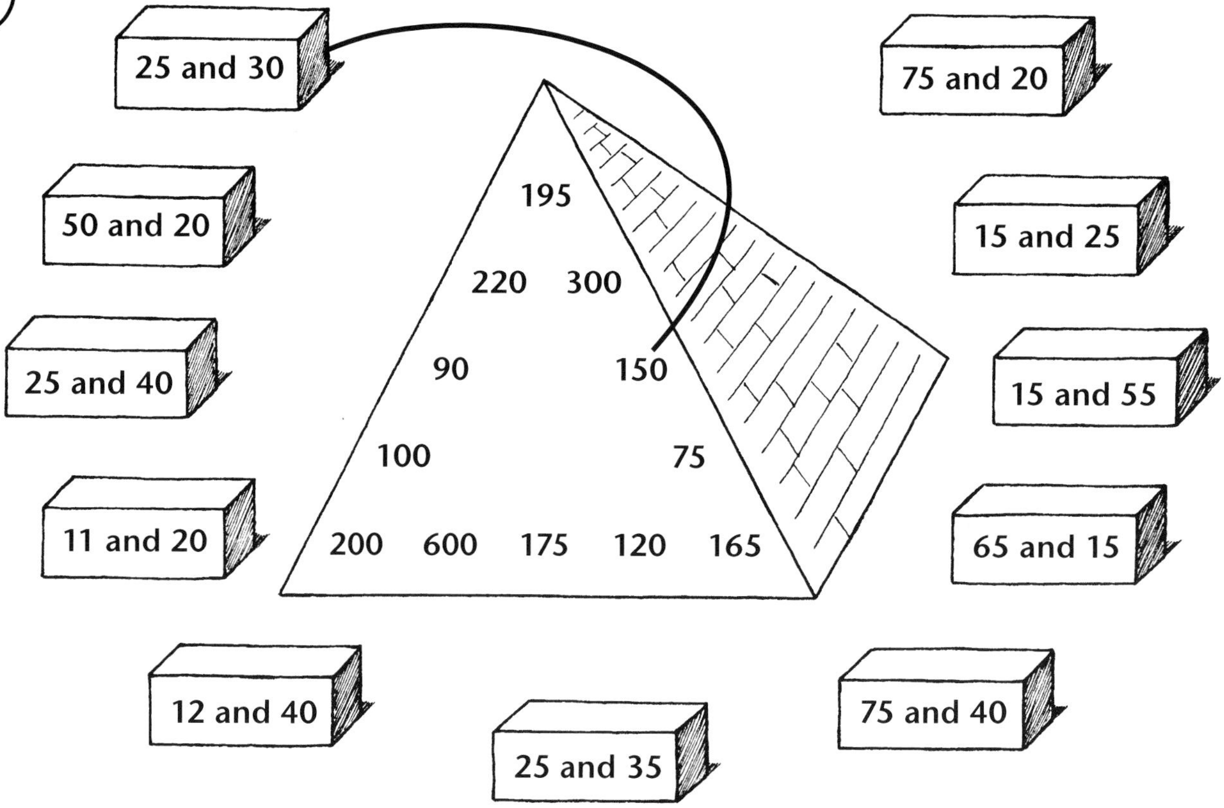

25 and 30 **75 and 20**

50 and 20 **15 and 25**

25 and 40 **15 and 55**

11 and 20 **65 and 15**

12 and 40 **25 and 35** **75 and 40**

195

220 **300**

90 **150**

100 **75**

200 **600** **175** **120** **165**

To find the **lowest common multiple**, list the first few multiples of each number until you find one that both numbers share: for example, to find the lowest common multiple of 25 and 30, list 25, 50, 75, 100, 125, 150... and 30, 60, 90, 120, 150... The first multiple that both 25 and 30 share is 150, so this is the lowest common multiple.

Special numbers

Recognise and use multiples and primes

1. Follow these instructions carefully.

- ☆ Colour the number 1 in the grid.
- ☆ Colour all the multiples of 2 (but *not* 2 itself)
- ☆ Next colour all the multiples of 3 (but *not* 3 itself)
- ☆ Then colour all the multiples of 4 (but *not* 4 itself)
- ☆ Keep going in the same way for multiples of 5, 6, 7, 8, 9 and 10, but remember *not* to colour the first multiple for each.

1	2	3	4	5	6	7	8	9	10
11	12	13	14	15	16	17	18	19	20
21	22	23	24	25	26	27	28	29	30
31	32	33	34	35	36	37	38	39	40
41	42	43	44	45	46	47	48	49	50
51	52	53	54	55	56	57	58	59	60
61	62	63	64	65	66	67	68	69	70
71	72	73	74	75	76	77	78	79	80
81	82	83	84	85	86	87	88	89	90
91	92	93	94	95	96	97	98	99	100

2. List the numbers not coloured, in order.

____

These numbers are called **prime numbers**. A prime number is a number with only two factors, itself and 1.

3. Why does this method help you find prime numbers? ______________________________

____

NOW TRY THIS!

4 9 16 25 36 49 64 81 100

- Write each of the **square numbers** above as the sum of two prime numbers.

Example:

square = prime + prime
4 = 2 + 2

9 =	2 + 7	**49** =	______
16 =	______	**64** =	______
25 =	______	**81** =	______
36 =	______	**100** =	______

Remember that **square numbers** are made by multiplying a number by itself: for example, 25 is a square number because it is the answer to 5 × 5 or five squared; 81 is a square number because it is the answer to 9 × 9, or nine squared.

Factor bars

1. Write the factors of each number on the chocolate bar chunks. Where possible, write the factors in pairs. Draw an outline around the completed chunks.

(a) 16

1	16
2	8
4	

(b) 24

1	24
2	
3	
	6

(c) 36

(d) 48

(e) 25

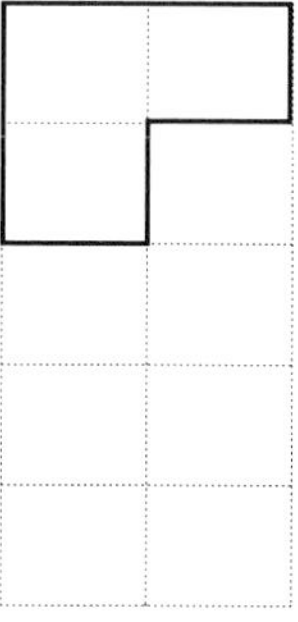

(f) 42

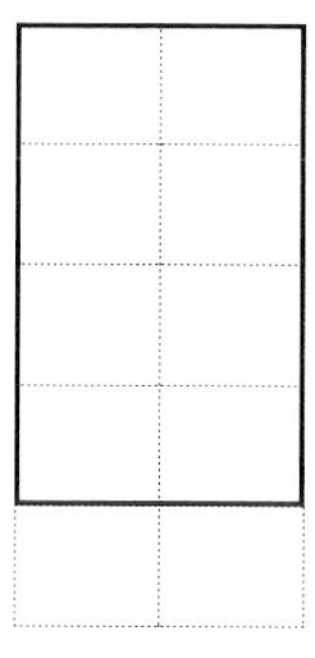

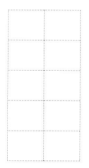

(g) 17

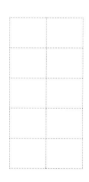

(h) 49

(i) 32

(j) 23

(k) 40

(l) 64

2. What do you notice about the number of factors of the **square numbers**?

3. Which **prime numbers** are shown above?

4. List six other prime numbers.

Circle the numbers which have exactly six factors, and complete the grids.

19 12 25 18 15 28 13 20 29

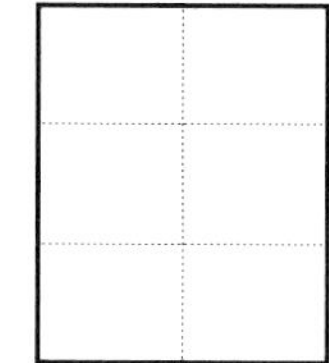

A **factor** is a number that divides exactly into another without a remainder. The number 10 has four factors: 1, 2, 5 and 10, as each of these numbers divides exactly into 10 without a remainder. Remember: a **square number** is made by multiplying a number by itself, and a **prime number** has only two factors – itself and 1.

Factor bars

Recognise and use factors and common factors

Look at the factors of 16 and 28.
The highest common factor is 4, as it is the highest factor that both numbers share.

1	16
2	8
4	

1	28
2	14
4	7

1. What is the highest common factor of:

(a) 16 and 24? ______ **(b)** 36 and 48? ______

(c) 16 and 32? ______ **(d)** 32 and 48? ______

(e) 42 and 40? ______ **(f)** 36 and 64? ______

(g) 40 and 28? ______ **(h)** 64 and 18? ______

(i) 48 and 20? ______ **(j)** 25 and 40? ______

(k) 42 and 36? ______ **(l)** 42 and 16? ______

(m) 32 and 28? ______ **(n)** 64 and 23? ______

Zara uses highest common factors to help her cancel fractions to their **simplest form**, like this:

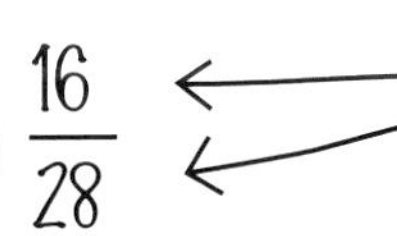

$\frac{16}{28}$ ← The highest common factor is 4, so I divide both numbers by 4.

$\frac{16 \div 4}{28 \div 4} = \frac{4}{7}$ ← The fraction in its simplest form

2. Change these fractions to their simplest form.

(a) $\frac{16}{24} = \frac{2}{3}$ **(b)** $\frac{36}{48} =$ **(c)** $\frac{16}{32} =$ **(d)** $\frac{32}{48} =$

(e) $\frac{42}{40} =$ **(f)** $\frac{36}{64} =$ **(g)** $\frac{40}{28} =$ **(h)** $\frac{18}{64} =$

NOW TRY THIS!

- Which number between 0 and 100 has:

(a) the fewest factors? ______

(b) the most factors? ______

(c) exactly 12 factors? ______

Use what you know about different types of numbers to help you.

Remember that you can cancel fractions by dividing the numerator (top number) and the denominator (bottom number) by the same number, for example $\frac{12}{14} = \frac{6}{7}$ (divide each number by 2). A **fraction in its simplest form** is one that cannot be cancelled any further: for example, $\frac{3}{4}$ is in its simplest form because there is no number that will divide exactly into both 3 and 4.

Use simple tests of divisibility

Let's investigate

1. Add the digits of these **multiples of 3**.

(a) 10 323 → 1 + 0 + 3 + 2 + 3 = 9 (b) 1662 → ______

(c) 7524 → ______ (d) 8358 → ______

(e) 10 020 → ______ (f) 70 167 → ______

What do you notice about the sum of the digits of a multiple of 3?

______

Use this information to write five multiples of 3 between 40 000 and 60 000.

______

2. Add the digits of these **multiples of 9**.

(a) 60 246 → ______ (b) 46 629 → ______

(c) 7524 → ______ (d) 8361 → ______

(e) 10 080 → ______ (f) 8991 → ______

What do you notice about the sum of the digits of a multiple of 9?

______

Use this information to write five multiples of 9 between 40 000 and 60 000.

______

Use the flow diagram on the next sheet to help you complete these tables.

	Divisible by							
Number	**2**	**3**	**4**	**5**	**6**	**8**	**9**	**10**
46 701	✗	✓	✗	✗	✗	✗	✓	✗
124								
341								
5798								
6714								
7920								
1584								
9458								
2481								

	Divisible by							
Number	**2**	**3**	**4**	**5**	**6**	**8**	**9**	**10**
4570								
36 819								
13 842								
12 455								
27 058								
25 490								
406 012								
462 124								
901 080								

You will need the other sheet called *Let's investigate* to help you complete part B. Notice that you are not asked to find whether the numbers are divisible by 7. This is because it is difficult to tell whether a number is divisible by 7 without using a calculator or a written method.

Let's investigate

Use simple tests of divisibility

C

1. Choose a number. Follow the instructions in the flow diagram.

START

1

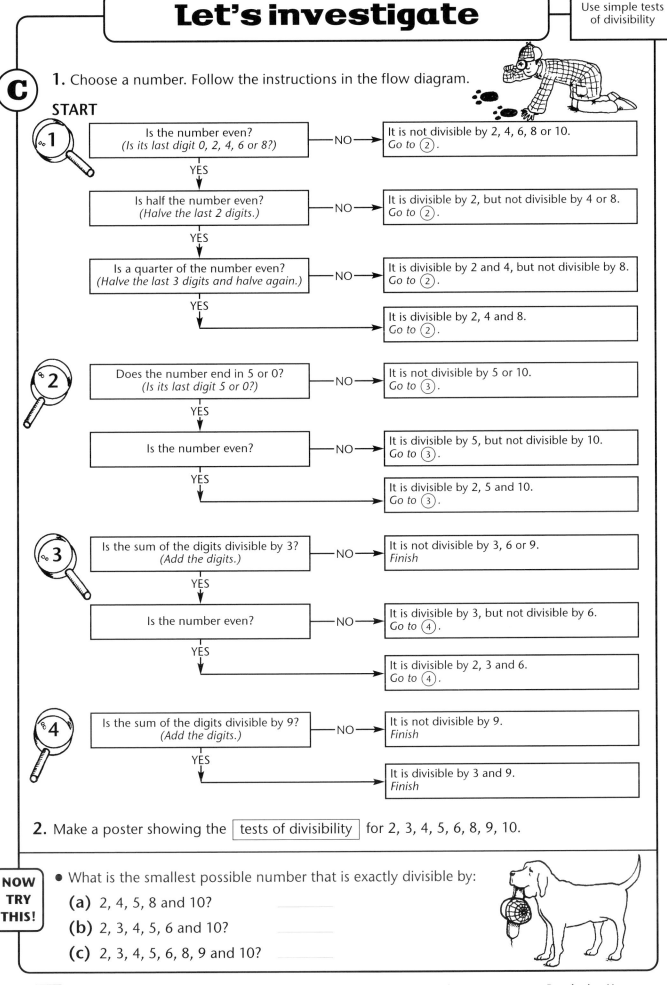

Question	If NO
Is the number even? *(Is its last digit 0, 2, 4, 6 or 8?)*	It is not divisible by 2, 4, 6, 8 or 10. *Go to* (2).
YES ↓ Is half the number even? *(Halve the last 2 digits.)*	It is divisible by 2, but not divisible by 4 or 8. *Go to* (2).
YES ↓ Is a quarter of the number even? *(Halve the last 3 digits and halve again.)*	It is divisible by 2 and 4, but not divisible by 8. *Go to* (2).
YES →	It is divisible by 2, 4 and 8. *Go to* (2).

2

Question	If NO
Does the number end in 5 or 0? *(Is its last digit 5 or 0?)*	It is not divisible by 5 or 10. *Go to* (3).
YES ↓ Is the number even?	It is divisible by 5, but not divisible by 10. *Go to* (3).
YES →	It is divisible by 2, 5 and 10. *Go to* (3).

3

Question	If NO
Is the sum of the digits divisible by 3? *(Add the digits.)*	It is not divisible by 3, 6 or 9. *Finish*
YES ↓ Is the number even?	It is divisible by 3, but not divisible by 6. *Go to* (4).
YES →	It is divisible by 2, 3 and 6. *Go to* (4).

4

Question	If NO
Is the sum of the digits divisible by 9? *(Add the digits.)*	It is not divisible by 9. *Finish*
YES →	It is divisible by 3 and 9. *Finish*

2. Make a poster showing the tests of divisibility for 2, 3, 4, 5, 6, 8, 9, 10.

NOW TRY THIS!

- What is the smallest possible number that is exactly divisible by:

(a) 2, 4, 5, 8 and 10? ______

(b) 2, 3, 4, 5, 6 and 10? ______

(c) 2, 3, 4, 5, 6, 8, 9 and 10? ______

This sheet shows you **tests of divisibility** for 2, 3, 4, 5, 6, 8, 9 and 10. If you wish to test for other numbers, use a calculator to divide. If the answer is a whole number, it is divisible by the number you tested.

Use triangular and square numbers, and square roots

Spot it!

1. Write the number of spots in each shape.

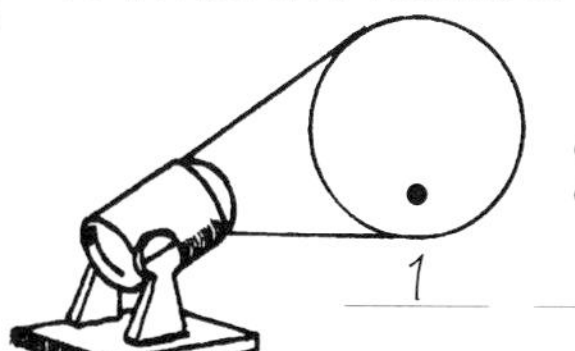

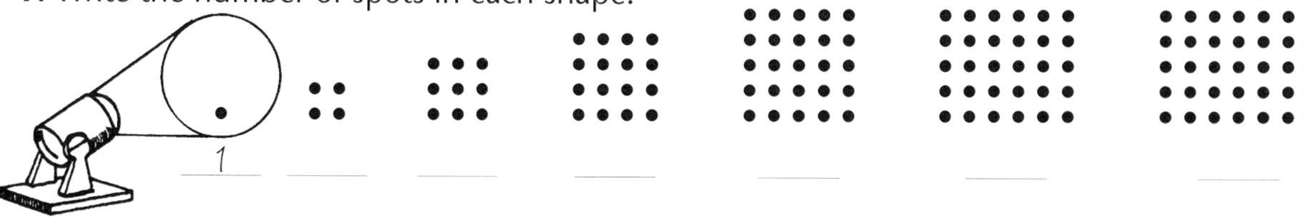

2. Write the next five square numbers. ____________________

3. Find the **difference** between pairs of adjacent square numbers.

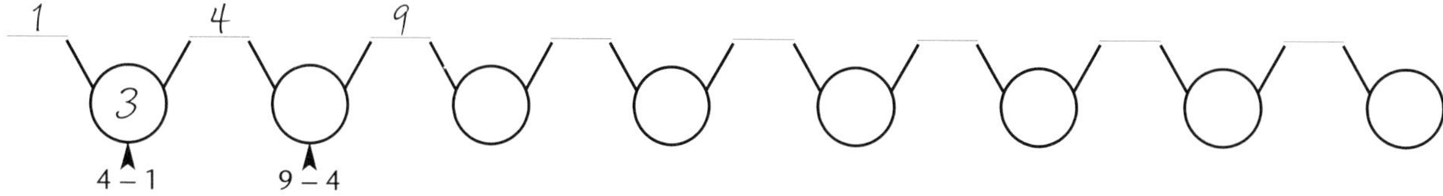

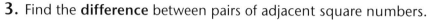

Write in words what you notice. ____________________

4. Write the number of spots in each shape.

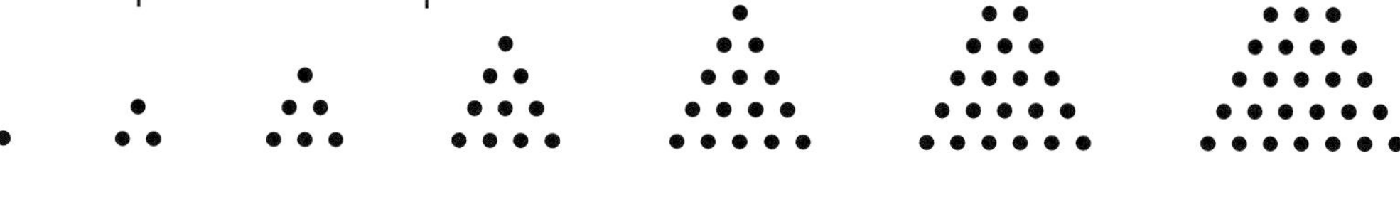

5. Write the next five triangular numbers. ____________________

6. Find the **difference** between pairs of adjacent triangular numbers.

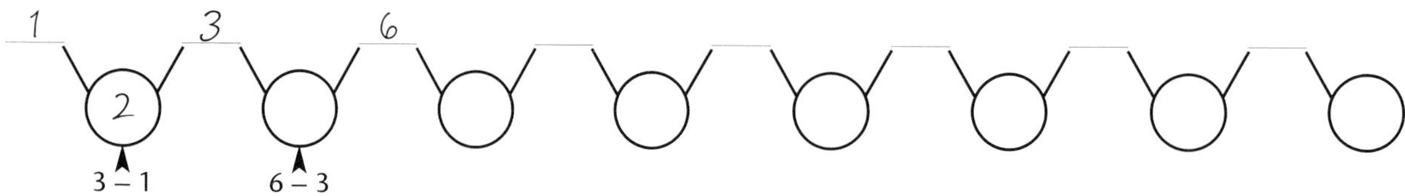

Write in words what you notice. ____________________

7. Find the **sum** of pairs of adjacent triangular numbers.

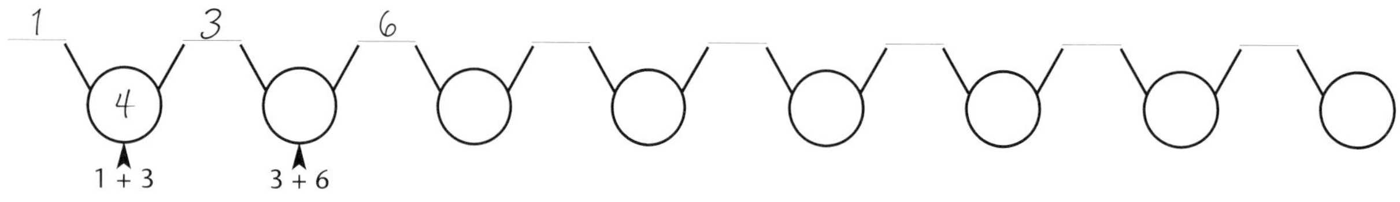

Write in words what you notice. ____________________

Join the equivalent values.

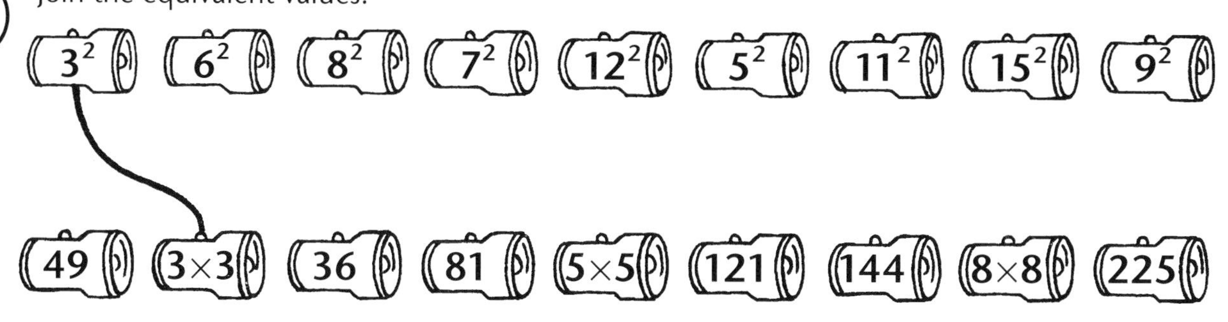

Remember that **square numbers** are made by multiplying a number by itself: for example, 3^2 (three squared) means 3 multiplied by itself, or 3×3, and is equal to 9. Make sure you know the first 12 square numbers by heart and learn the first six triangular numbers.

Spot it!

Use triangular and square numbers, and square roots

1. How many spots are there along each side of a square if it has:

(a) 16 spots? 4 **(b)** 36 spots? ______

(c) 64 spots? ______ **(d)** 49 spots? ______

(e) 100 spots? ______ **(f)** 144 spots? ______

(g) 1600 spots? ______ **(h)** 2500 spots? ______

(i) 90 000 spots? ______

2. Write the questions and answers above using the square root sign.

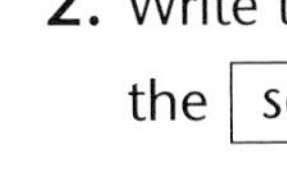
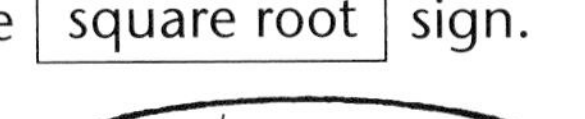
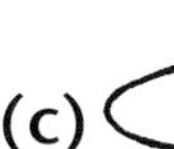

(a) $\sqrt{16} = 4$ **(b)** ______ **(c)** ______

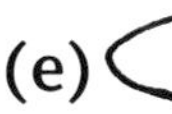

(d) ______ **(e)** ______ **(f)** ______

(g) ______ **(h)** ______ **(i)** ______

3. Complete this crossnumber puzzle.

1 2	4	2 8	(shaded)	3
	(shaded)		(shaded)	
4	5		6	(shaded)
(shaded)		(shaded)	7	
8				(shaded)

Across

1. Thirty-three squared subtract twenty-nine squared.
4. $90^2 + 18^2 + 3^2$
7. $\sqrt{7225}$
8. $95^2 - 2^2$

Down

1. $17^2 + 3^2$
2. 5 squared plus 27 squared plus 7 squared.
3. $\sqrt{8100}$
5. $\sqrt{160\,000}$
6. $21^2 - \sqrt{3600}$

NOW TRY THIS!

- Work with a partner. Use these cards to make at least 20 different true statements. You may use each digit more than once.

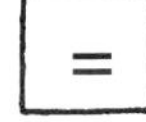 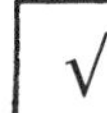 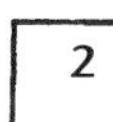      

= √ ² 0 1 3 6 8 9

Examples: $19^2 = 361$ $\sqrt{900} = 30$

Remember that squaring and finding the **square root** are the inverse (opposite) of each other, so a squaring statement can be written the other way round as a square root statement: for example, $3^2 = 9$ and $\sqrt{9} = 3$.

Express one number as a fraction of another

Fraction distraction

1. What fraction of each circle is shaded?

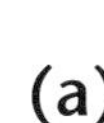

(a) 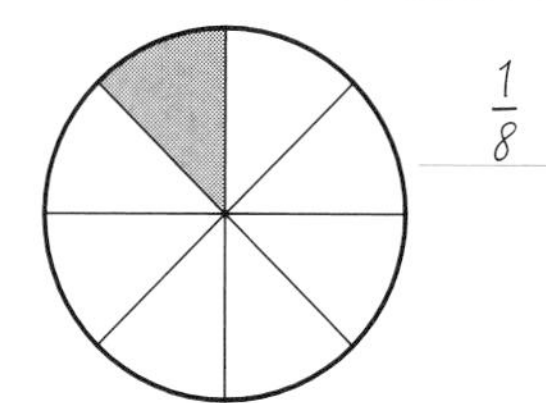 $\frac{1}{8}$

(b) 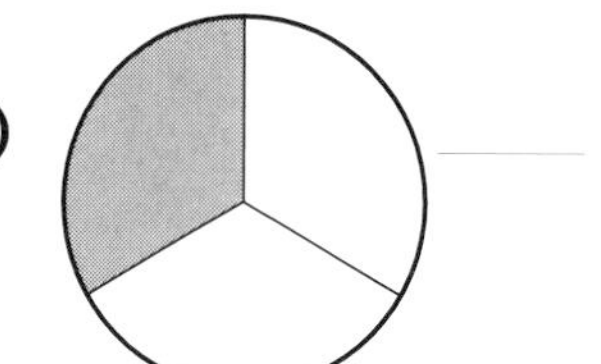

(c) 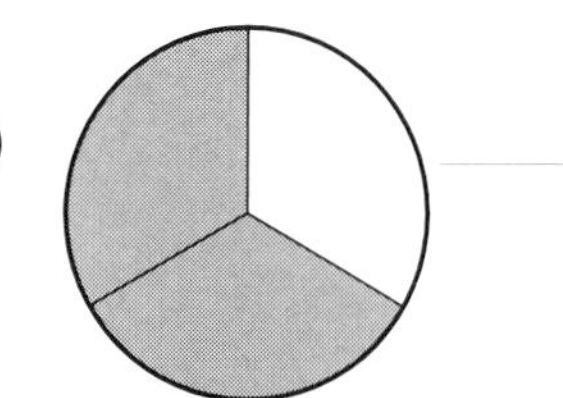

(d) 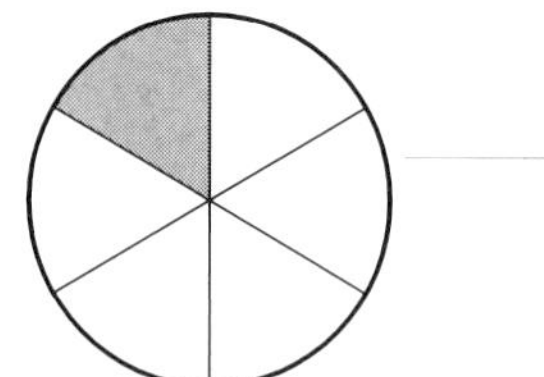

(e) 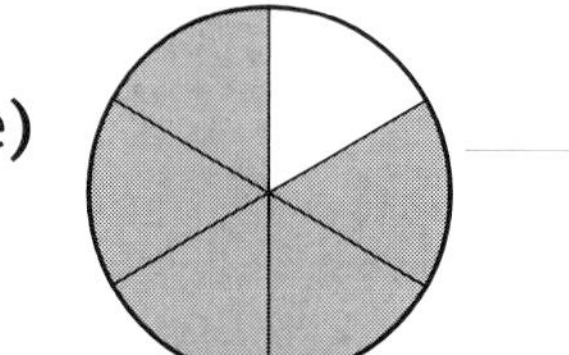

(f) 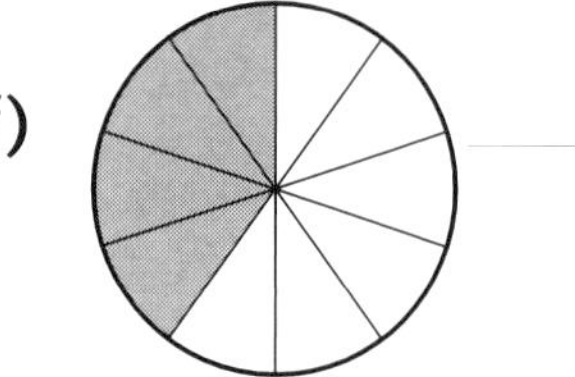

(g) 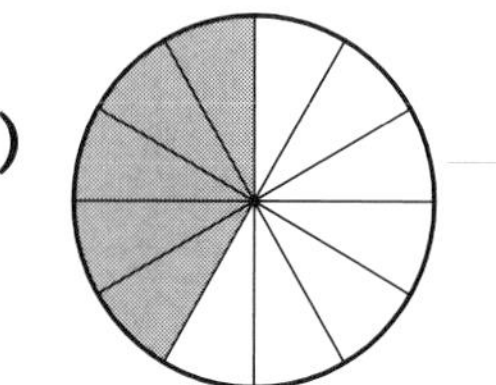

(h) 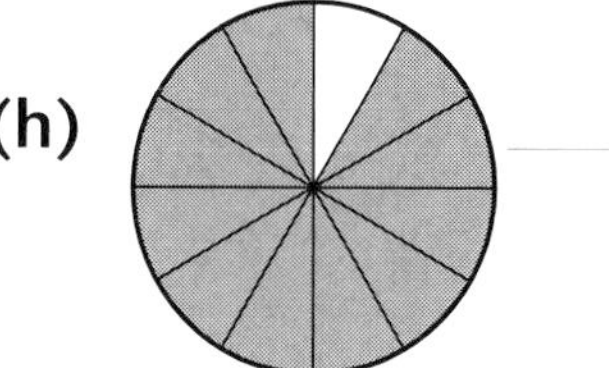

(i) 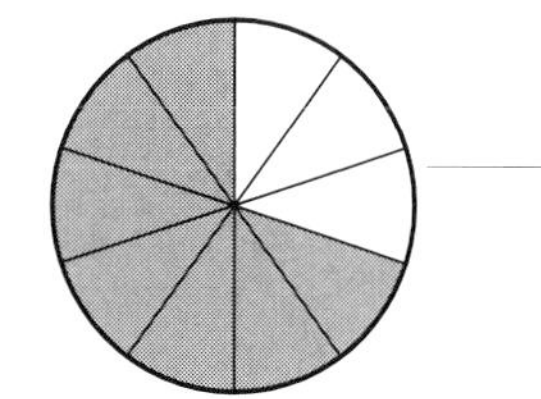

2. Write the fractions above in order of size, starting with the smallest.

Look at the circles above to help you.

 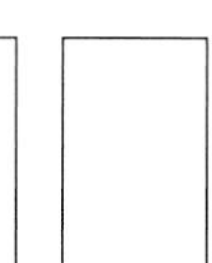  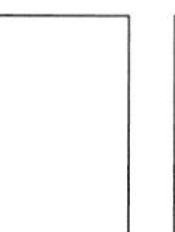 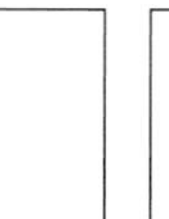 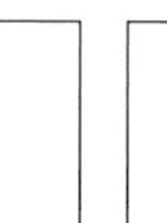 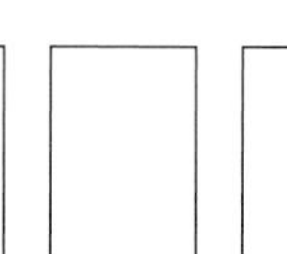

3. What fraction of a complete turn does the minute hand of a clock turn through between:

(a) 10:00 and 10:15? $\frac{15}{60} = \frac{1}{4}$

(b) 10:00 and 10:20? ______

(c) 8:15 and 8:45? ______

(d) 7:30 and 7:40? ______

(e) 5:00 and 5:40? ______

(f) 3:05 and 3:50? ______

(g) 1:40 and 1:45? ______

(h) 12:05 and 12:55? ______

(i) 9:10 and 10:00? ______

(j) 2:15 and 2:40? ______

(k) 6:20 and 6:55? ______

(l) 4:15 and 4:16? ______

B

Alex is thinking of two times between 4:00 pm and 5:00 pm.
Between the two times the minute hand turns $\frac{7}{12}$ of a complete turn.
Find six pairs of times that Alex could be thinking of.

4:20 pm and 4:55 pm

Remember that the number on the bottom of a fraction, called the denominator, tells you how many equal parts the whole is split into. The number on the top, called the numerator, is how many of those parts you are talking about. In A3, give your answers in their simplest form (divide the numerator and the denominator by the same number, if you can).

Fraction distraction

Express one number as a fraction of another

A company makes capital letters for signs. Each letter is cut from a square metal sheet like the one on the right.

1. What fraction of a whole sheet is used for each of these letters?

(a) 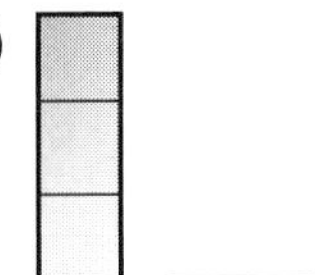 ______ (b) 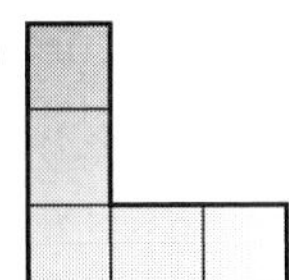 ______ (c) 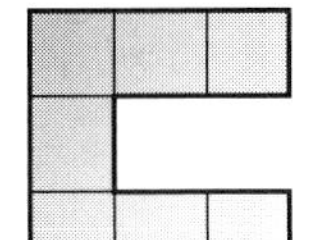 ______ (d) 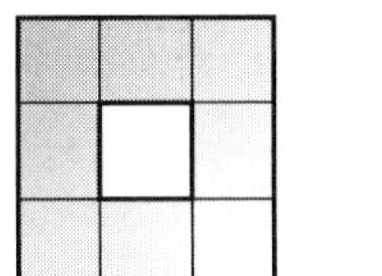 ______

(e) 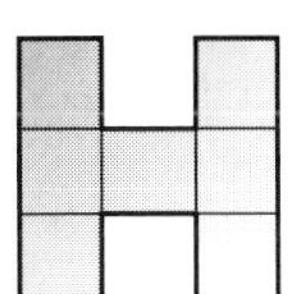 ______ (f) 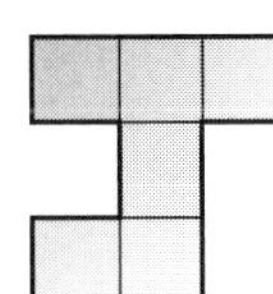 ______ (g) 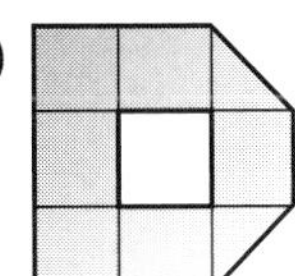 ______ (h) 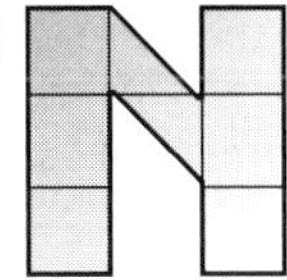 ______

2. Shade other capital letters on the templates below. Write what fraction of the whole sheet is used for each letter.

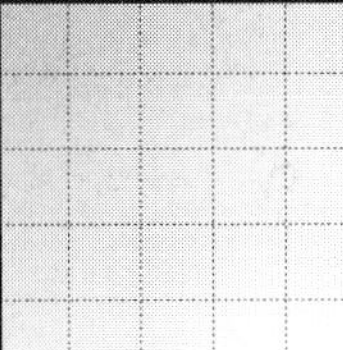

(a)  ______ (b) 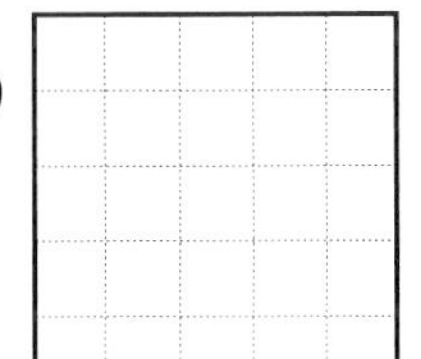 ______ (c)  ______

(d)  ______ (e) 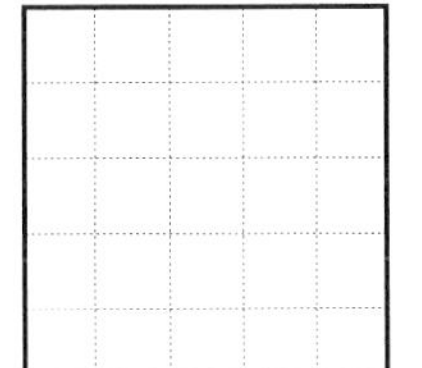 ______ (f)  ______

(g) 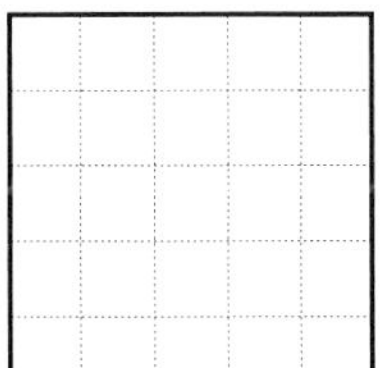 ______ (h) 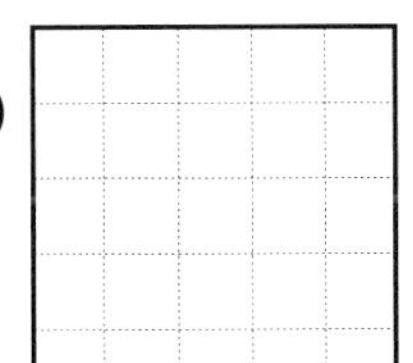 ______ (i)  ______

NOW TRY THIS!

- If there are 24 sweets in a bag, what fraction (in its simplest form) of the sweets is:

(a) 12 sweets? ______ **(b)** 6 sweets? ______ **(c)** 7 sweets? ______

(d) 8 sweets? ______ **(e)** 3 sweets? ______ **(f)** 14 sweets? ______

(g) 16 sweets? ______ **(h)** 9 sweets? ______ **(i)** 23 sweets? ______

Write all the fractions in their simplest form. To give a smaller number as a fraction of a larger one, remember that the larger number will be the denominator (bottom number) and the smaller number will be the numerator (top number). Then cancel the fraction to its simplest form (divide the numerator and the denominator by the same number, if you can).

Identify equivalent fractions and decimals

Equivalence

Shade two diagrams in each set to show equivalent fractions. Record as proper fractions.

(a)
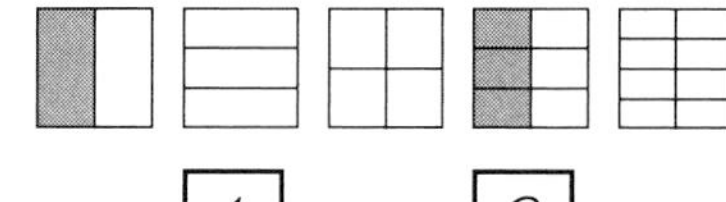

$\frac{1}{2} = \frac{3}{6}$

(b)
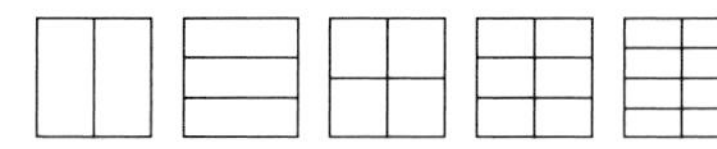

$\frac{\square}{\square} = \frac{\square}{\square}$

(c)
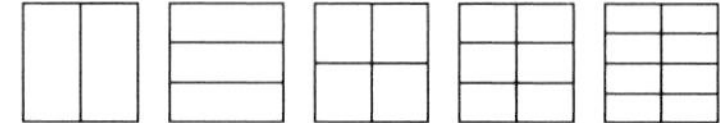

$\frac{\square}{\square} = \frac{\square}{\square}$

(d)
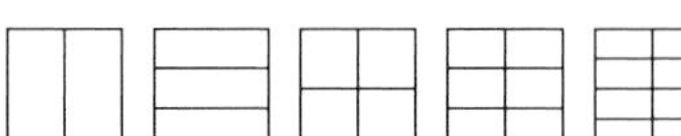

$\frac{\square}{\square} = \frac{\square}{\square}$

(e)
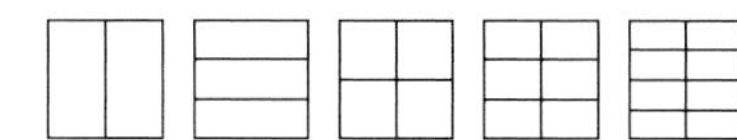

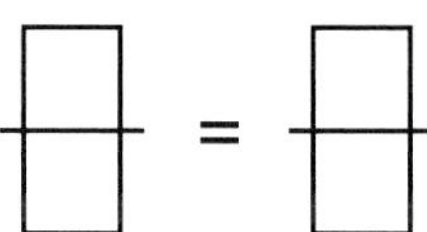

$\frac{\square}{\square} = \frac{\square}{\square}$

(f)
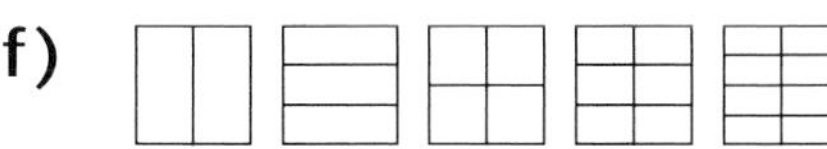

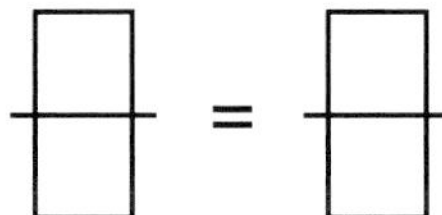

$\frac{\square}{\square} = \frac{\square}{\square}$

1. Read Jo's instructions for using the multiplication square.

1	2	3	4	5	6	7	8	9	10
2	4	6	8	10	12	14	16	18	20
3	6	9	12	15	18	21	24	27	30
4	8	12	16	20	24	28	32	36	40
5	10	15	20	25	30	35	40	45	50
6	12	18	24	30	36	42	48	54	60
7	14	21	28	35	42	49	56	63	70
8	16	24	32	40	48	56	64	72	80
9	18	27	36	45	54	63	72	81	90
10	20	30	40	50	60	70	80	90	100

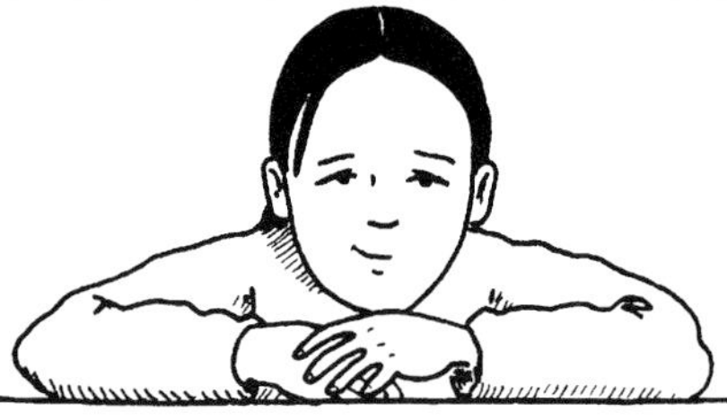

☆ **Step 1** Choose two numbers from the same column to form a proper fraction.

☆ **Step 2** Look at the number at the top of the column to find out which table both numbers are in.

☆ **Step 3** Divide both numbers by this table number to change your fraction to an equivalent fraction in a simpler form.

$$\frac{27 \div 9}{72 \div 9} = \frac{3}{8}$$

☆ **Step 4** Look across the grid from the numbers you chose, to the two numbers in the left-hand column.

2. Write 20 fractions and their equivalents by following Jo's instructions.

$\frac{8}{28} = \frac{2}{7}$,

3. Tick the fractions which are in their simplest form.

Equivalent means 'equal in value'. Remember that a **proper fraction** is one in which the denominator (bottom number) is larger than the numerator (top number). Proper fractions are always less than 1.

Equivalence

Identify equivalent fractions and decimals

$\frac{1}{20}$	$\frac{3}{5}$	$\frac{1}{5}$	$\frac{1}{100}$	$\frac{3}{10}$	$\frac{1}{10}$	$\frac{7}{20}$	$\frac{99}{100}$	$\frac{19}{20}$	$\frac{3}{4}$	$\frac{4}{5}$	$\frac{29}{100}$	$\frac{9}{10}$
A	N	E	J	B	M	O	M	L	D	F	S	I

1. Write each decimal as a fraction in its simplest form. Then use the key above to find the code letter for each answer.

(a) 0.6 = $\frac{6}{10} = \frac{3}{5}$ [N]

(b) 0.3 = ________ [ ]

(c) 0.75 = ________ [ ]

(d) 0.05 = ________ [ ]

(e) 0.1 = ________ [ ]

(f) 0.99 = ________ [ ]

(g) 0.01 = ________ [ ]

(h) 0.90 = ________ [ ]

(i) 0.29 = ________ [ ]

(j) 0.35 = ________ [ ]

(k) 0.2 = ________ [ ]

(l) 0.95 = ________ [ ]

(m) 0.8 = ________ [ ]

2. Unscramble the letters of your answers to find out what Li watched on TV last night.
Clue: arrange the answers in **ascending order**.

J

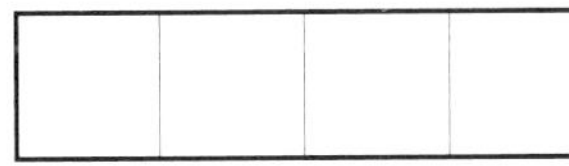

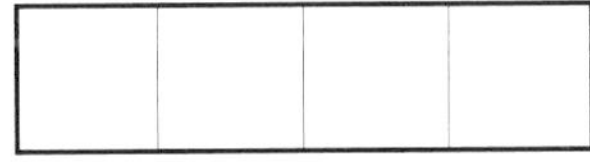

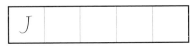

NOW TRY THIS!

1 2 3 5 7 0 .

- Use these cards to make at least 20 decimals that have two or three decimal places and are less than 1. For each decimal, write an equivalent fraction in its simplest form.

Example: $0.125 = \frac{125}{1000} = \frac{1}{8}$

To change a fraction to its simplest form, divide the numerator (top number) and the denominator (bottom number) by the same number. This gives an equivalent fraction. If there is no number that will divide exactly into both the numbers, the fraction is in its simplest form. **Ascending order** means in order from smallest to largest.

Compare two or more fractions

Fraction Friction

1. The Fractious twins are arguing about fractions! Using the fraction board to help you, tick to show who is correct. Write each true statement using the <, > or = sign.

$\frac{1}{2}$	$\frac{1}{2}$								
$\frac{1}{3}$	$\frac{1}{3}$	$\frac{1}{3}$							
$\frac{1}{4}$	$\frac{1}{4}$	$\frac{1}{4}$	$\frac{1}{4}$						
$\frac{1}{5}$	$\frac{1}{5}$	$\frac{1}{5}$	$\frac{1}{5}$	$\frac{1}{5}$					
$\frac{1}{6}$	$\frac{1}{6}$	$\frac{1}{6}$	$\frac{1}{6}$	$\frac{1}{6}$	$\frac{1}{6}$				
$\frac{1}{8}$	$\frac{1}{8}$	$\frac{1}{8}$	$\frac{1}{8}$	$\frac{1}{8}$	$\frac{1}{8}$	$\frac{1}{8}$	$\frac{1}{8}$		
$\frac{1}{10}$	$\frac{1}{10}$	$\frac{1}{10}$	$\frac{1}{10}$	$\frac{1}{10}$	$\frac{1}{10}$	$\frac{1}{10}$	$\frac{1}{10}$	$\frac{1}{10}$	$\frac{1}{10}$

(a) Two-fifths is less than one half. ✔ $\frac{2}{5} < \frac{1}{2}$ No, two-fifths is greater than one half. ☐

(b) Five-eighths is less than three-quarters. ☐ ______ No, five-eighths is greater than three-quarters. ☐

(c) Five-sixths is greater than seven-eighths. ☐ ______ No, five-sixths is less than seven-eighths. ☐

(d) Four-tenths is the same as two-fifths. ☐ ______ No, four-tenths is greater than two-fifths. ☐

(e) Eight-tenths is less than three-quarters. ☐ ______ No, eight-tenths is greater than three-quarters. ☐

(f) Two-thirds is greater than five-eighths. ☐ ______ No, two-thirds is less than five-eighths. ☐

2. Circle the fractions which are more than one half.

$\frac{2}{3}$ $\frac{3}{5}$ $\frac{3}{8}$ $\frac{4}{5}$ $\frac{5}{8}$ $\frac{2}{5}$ $\frac{1}{6}$ $\frac{4}{6}$ $\frac{5}{6}$ $\frac{1}{3}$ $\frac{4}{10}$ $\frac{6}{10}$ $\frac{7}{8}$

Fill in the <, > or = sign to make true statements.

Use the fraction board to help you.

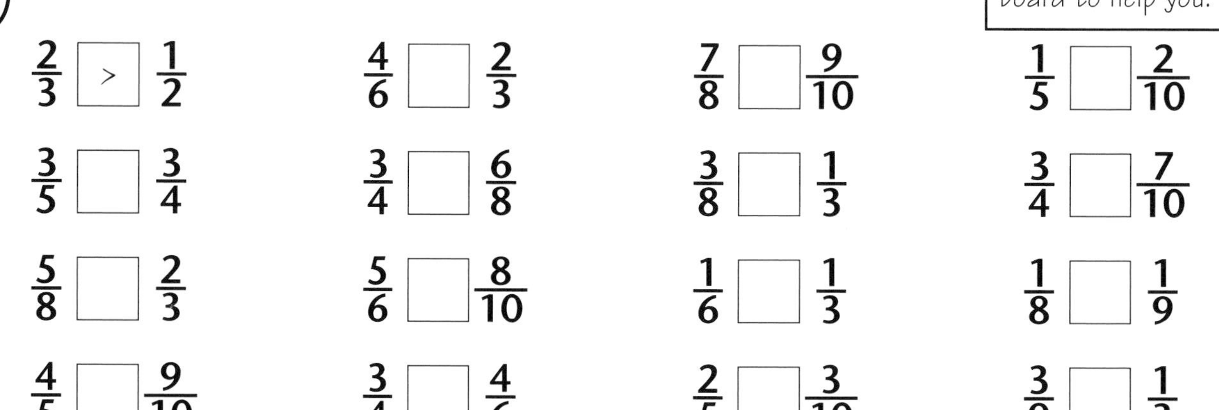

$\frac{2}{3}$ [>] $\frac{1}{2}$	$\frac{4}{6}$ [ ] $\frac{2}{3}$	$\frac{7}{8}$ [ ] $\frac{9}{10}$	$\frac{1}{5}$ [ ] $\frac{2}{10}$
$\frac{3}{5}$ [ ] $\frac{3}{4}$	$\frac{3}{4}$ [ ] $\frac{6}{8}$	$\frac{3}{8}$ [ ] $\frac{1}{3}$	$\frac{3}{4}$ [ ] $\frac{7}{10}$
$\frac{5}{8}$ [ ] $\frac{2}{3}$	$\frac{5}{6}$ [ ] $\frac{8}{10}$	$\frac{1}{6}$ [ ] $\frac{1}{3}$	$\frac{1}{8}$ [ ] $\frac{1}{9}$
$\frac{4}{5}$ [ ] $\frac{9}{10}$	$\frac{3}{4}$ [ ] $\frac{4}{6}$	$\frac{2}{5}$ [ ] $\frac{3}{10}$	$\frac{3}{9}$ [ ] $\frac{1}{3}$

Remember that for a fraction with a large denominator (bottom number), each part is smaller than in a fraction with a small denominator: for example, $\frac{1}{10}$ is smaller than $\frac{1}{5}$.

Fraction Friction

Compare two or more fractions

C

1. Read how Alex answered this question.

Which is smaller?
($\frac{3}{8}$ circled) or $\frac{2}{5}$

I think $\frac{3}{8}$ is smaller than $\frac{2}{5}$ because...
$\frac{3}{8}$ is equivalent to $\frac{15}{40}$.
$\frac{2}{5}$ is equivalent to $\frac{16}{40}$.
I know that $\frac{15}{40}$ is smaller than $\frac{16}{40}$.

Circle the correct answers. Explain how you know which fraction is smaller.

(a) Which is smaller? $\frac{5}{8}$ or $\frac{3}{5}$

(b) Which is smaller? $\frac{5}{6}$ or $\frac{4}{5}$

(c) Which is smaller? $\frac{3}{9}$ or $\frac{2}{5}$

2. Play this game with a partner.

- ☆ Each player chooses a fraction from the grid. Write the fractions down and cross them off the grid.
- ☆ Work out which fraction is larger.
- ☆ The player with the larger fraction scores a point.

$\frac{5}{6}$	$\frac{8}{9}$	$\frac{3}{8}$	$\frac{6}{7}$	$\frac{5}{8}$	$\frac{1}{3}$	$\frac{7}{8}$	$\frac{2}{5}$
$\frac{9}{10}$	$\frac{4}{5}$	$\frac{2}{5}$	$\frac{4}{3}$	$\frac{8}{10}$	$\frac{5}{10}$	$\frac{2}{3}$	$\frac{4}{7}$
$\frac{5}{7}$	$\frac{1}{2}$	$\frac{1}{6}$	$\frac{3}{3}$	$\frac{8}{9}$	$\frac{4}{9}$	$\frac{6}{10}$	$\frac{2}{7}$

Take turns to choose first! **!**

NOW TRY THIS!

- Use two different digits to make a **proper fraction**. Now write an improper fraction using the same digits. Which of the two fractions is closer to 1?

Example: $\frac{5}{7}$ is two-sevenths away from 1, and $\frac{7}{5}$ is two-fifths away from 1. So $\frac{5}{7}$ is closer to 1.

- Do this ten times.
- Write a rule to explain which fraction is closer to 1 each time.

To change a fraction to an equivalent one, simply multiply or divide the numerator and denominator by the same number. Remember that a **proper fraction** is one in which the denominator (bottom number) is larger than the numerator (top number). An **improper fraction** is one in which the numerator is larger than the denominator.

Add and subtract simple fractions

Fraction frenzy

1. Mark Holly's homework with a ✔ or a ✗ and correct her mistakes.

Holly Berry

(a) $\frac{1}{3}+\frac{1}{3}+\frac{1}{3}=\frac{3}{4}$ ✗ 1

(b) $\frac{1}{4}+\frac{1}{2}+\frac{1}{4}=1$

(c) $\frac{1}{5}+\frac{3}{5}+\frac{2}{5}=1$

(d) $\frac{1}{4}+\frac{1}{2}+\frac{3}{4}=1\frac{3}{4}$

(e) $\frac{2}{6}+\frac{2}{6}+\frac{5}{6}=1\frac{1}{2}$

(f) $\frac{1}{5}+\frac{1}{5}+\frac{2}{5}=\frac{4}{5}$

(g) $\frac{1}{8}+\frac{3}{8}+\frac{5}{8}=1$

(h) $\frac{2}{10}+\frac{1}{10}+\frac{2}{10}=\frac{1}{2}$

(i) $\frac{2}{4}+\frac{1}{2}+\frac{3}{4}=1\frac{1}{2}$

(j) $\frac{1}{9}+\frac{5}{9}+\frac{3}{9}=1$

(k) $\frac{2}{3}+\frac{2}{3}+\frac{2}{3}=2$

(l) $\frac{3}{4}+\frac{3}{4}+\frac{3}{4}=2$

(m) $\frac{4}{5}+\frac{4}{5}+\frac{2}{5}=2$

(n) $\frac{3}{8}+\frac{7}{8}+\frac{7}{8}=2\frac{1}{2}$

(o) $\frac{5}{6}+\frac{3}{6}+\frac{5}{6}=2$

(p) $\frac{1}{4}+\frac{2}{8}+\frac{2}{8}=\frac{3}{4}$

(q) $\frac{1}{3}+\frac{2}{6}+\frac{2}{6}=1$

(r) $\frac{1}{2}+\frac{5}{10}+\frac{1}{3}=1\frac{1}{3}$

2. On each line, write a set of three fractions that have a total of 1.

Try to use at least two fractions with different denominators. **!**

$\frac{1}{10}+\frac{1}{2}+\frac{4}{10}=1$

B Tick the pairs of fractions that have a difference of $\frac{2}{5}$.

$\frac{3}{5}$ ✔ $\frac{1}{5}$	$\frac{6}{5}$ ☐ $\frac{3}{5}$	$\frac{7}{10}$ ☐ $\frac{3}{10}$	$\frac{7}{5}$ ☐ $\frac{5}{5}$
$\frac{1}{10}$ ☐ $\frac{3}{10}$	$\frac{3}{5}$ ☐ $\frac{2}{10}$	$\frac{4}{5}$ ☐ $\frac{2}{5}$	$\frac{1}{5}$ ☐ $\frac{6}{10}$
$\frac{2}{10}$ ☐ $\frac{4}{5}$	$\frac{8}{5}$ ☐ $\frac{6}{5}$	$\frac{3}{15}$ ☐ $\frac{3}{5}$	$\frac{9}{10}$ ☐ $\frac{1}{2}$

Remember that it is easier to add fractions that have the same denominator (bottom number), so change the fractions to equivalent ones so that the denominators are all the same. Then all you need to do is add the numerators (top numbers) and change the answer to its simplest form.

Fraction frenzy

Add and subtract simple fractions

C Play these games with a partner. You each need a copy of this sheet and a counter. You also need a dice.

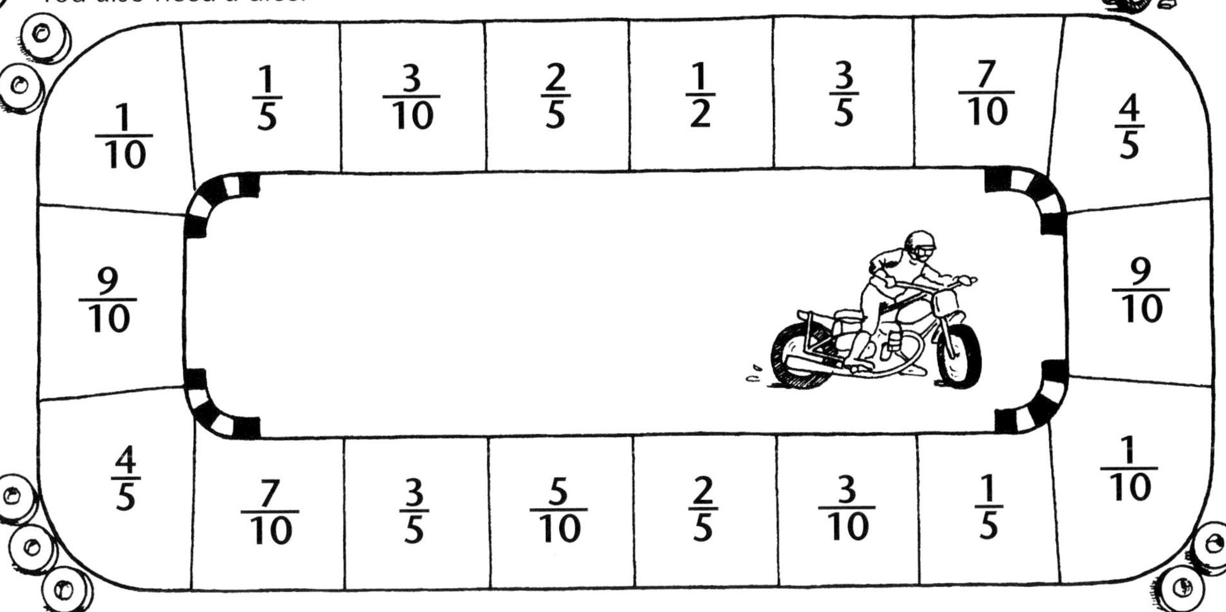

Game 1:
- ☆ Place your counter anywhere on the track above.
- ☆ Take turns to roll the dice and move in a clockwise direction. Keep a record of the fractions you land on.
- ☆ Score a point each time that you can make a total of 1 exactly, with two or more of your fractions. Continue until you have filled all the boxes.

My fractions													

Game 2: ☆ Play the game as above, but score a point each time that you can make a total of $1\frac{1}{2}$, with two or more of your fractions.

My fractions													

Game 3: ☆ As above, but score a point for each pair of fractions with a difference of three-tenths.

My fractions													

NOW TRY THIS!

- Arrange these fractions so that each row, diagonal and column has a total of $1\frac{1}{2}$.

$\frac{9}{10}$ ~~$\frac{1}{2}$~~ ~~$\frac{3}{10}$~~ ~~$\frac{1}{5}$~~ $\frac{2}{5}$ $\frac{3}{5}$ $\frac{4}{5}$ $\frac{1}{10}$ $\frac{7}{10}$

	$\frac{3}{10}$	
	$\frac{1}{2}$	
$\frac{1}{5}$		

Remember: $1\frac{1}{2}$ is equivalent to $1\frac{5}{10}$ and $\frac{15}{10}$.

Remember that $\frac{2}{10}$ is equivalent to $\frac{1}{5}$, $\frac{4}{10}$ is equivalent to $\frac{2}{5}$, and so on. Also note that improper fractions (ones in which the numerator is larger than the denominator) can be changed into mixed numbers, for example $\frac{8}{5} = 1\frac{3}{5}$.

Calculate fractions of quantities or measurements

Fraction partitions

1. Mrs Wilson puts her class into groups. There are 36 pupils in the class. Write how many pupils are in each group.

(a) Group A is $\frac{1}{6}$ of the class = 6 pupils

(b) Group B is $\frac{2}{9}$ of the class = ______ pupils

(c) Group C is $\frac{4}{12}$ of the class = ______ pupils

(d) Group D is $\frac{3}{18}$ of the class = ______ pupils

(e) What fraction of the class are in the remaining group (group E)? ______

2. There are 90 Year 7 pupils at Eskdale School. How many pupils are in each sports team?

(a) Team A is $\frac{1}{10}$ of Year 7 = ______ pupils

(b) Team B is $\frac{2}{9}$ of Year 7 = ______ pupils

(c) Team C is $\frac{2}{5}$ of Year 7 = ______ pupils

(d) Team D is $\frac{2}{15}$ of Year 7 = ______ pupils

(e) Team E is $\frac{4}{45}$ of Year 7 = ______ pupils

(f) What fraction of Year 7 are in the remaining team (Team F)? ______

3. There are 224 pupils at River Primary School. How many pupils are in each class?

(a) Reception has $\frac{1}{4}$ of the pupils = ______ pupils

(b) Class 1 has $\frac{1}{14}$ of the pupils = ______ pupils

(c) Class 2 has $\frac{3}{28}$ of the pupils = ______ pupils

(d) Class 3 has $\frac{1}{7}$ of the pupils = ______ pupils

(e) Class 4 has $\frac{3}{56}$ of the pupils = ______ pupils

(f) Classes 5 and 6 together have $\frac{3}{8}$ of the pupils = ______ pupils

B

Write the answers.

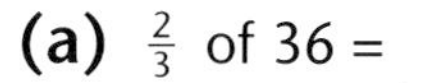

(a) $\frac{2}{3}$ of 36 = ______	**(b)** $\frac{5}{8}$ of 24 = ______	**(c)** $\frac{5}{6}$ of 42 = ______
(d) $\frac{4}{9}$ of 45 = ______	**(e)** $\frac{5}{7}$ of 49 = ______	**(f)** $\frac{7}{8}$ of 56 = ______
(g) $\frac{5}{9}$ of 72 = ______	**(h)** $\frac{4}{5}$ of 75 = ______	**(i)** $\frac{3}{7}$ of 77 = ______

To answer a question such as 'find $\frac{4}{5}$ of 35', first find one-fifth by dividing by 5. Once you know what one-fifth is, you can find four-fifths by multiplying by 4.

Fraction partitions

Calculate fractions of quantities or measurements

C

1. (a) Start with a multiple of 6 and follow the trail. For each step, use your answer to the previous one. Record each stage of the trail. Follow the trail five times, each time starting with a different multiple of 6.

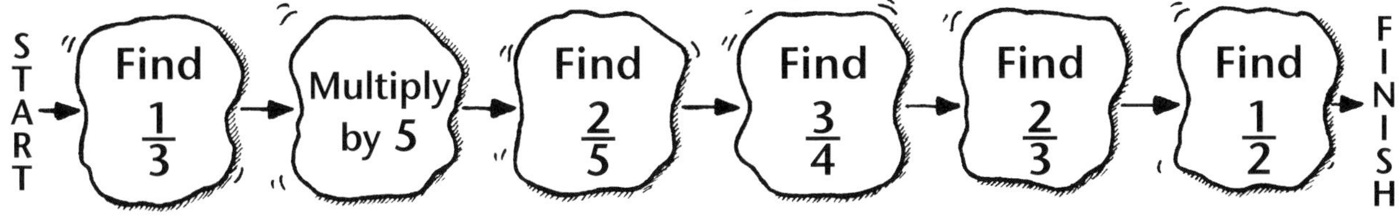

12	→	4	→	20	→	8	→	6	→	4	→	2

(b) Write what you notice about the start and finish numbers. ______________________

____

2. (a) Start with a multiple of 4 and follow this trail in the same way. Follow the trail five times, each time starting with a different multiple of 4.

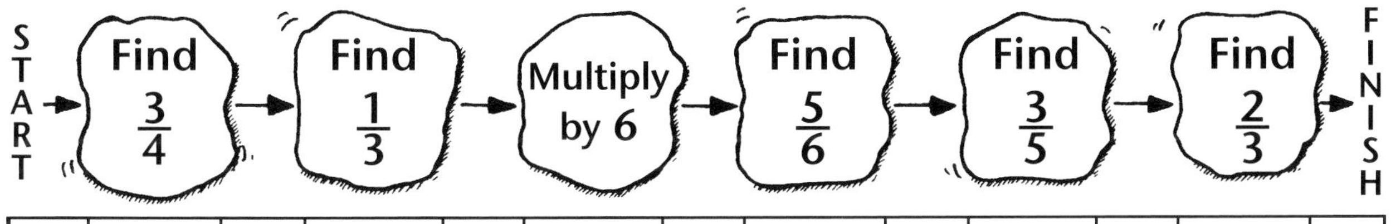

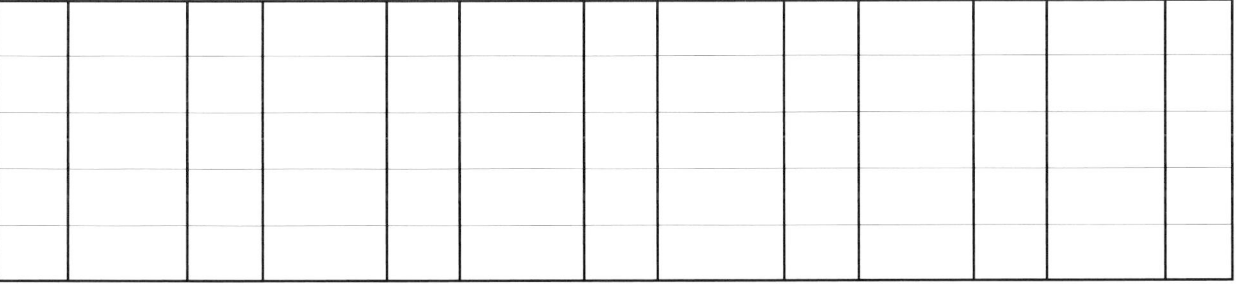

(b) Write what you notice about the start and finish numbers. ______________________

____

NOW TRY THIS!

- Make up your own trail where, if you start with the number 96, you will get a whole number answer to each question.

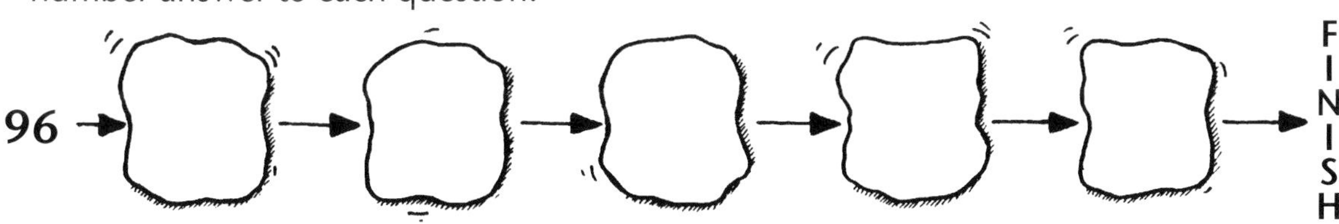

To answer a question such as 'find $\frac{4}{5}$ of 35', first find one-fifth by dividing by 5. Once you know what one-fifth is, you can find four-fifths by multiplying by 4.

Multiply fractions by integers, including mixed numbers

Fraction action

A Change these improper fractions to mixed numbers to complete the trail.

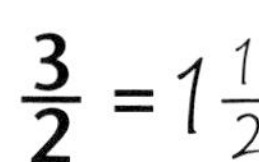

$\frac{3}{2} = 1\frac{1}{2}$

$\frac{8}{5} =$

$\frac{9}{4} =$

$\frac{15}{6} =$

$\frac{13}{10} =$

$\frac{27}{10} =$

$\frac{11}{5} =$

$\frac{13}{8} =$

$\frac{16}{5} =$

$\frac{7}{2} =$

$\frac{7}{3} =$

$\frac{25}{8} =$

$\frac{19}{5} =$

$\frac{17}{4} =$

$\frac{21}{3} =$

$\frac{23}{8} =$

$\frac{22}{5} =$

$\frac{15}{8} =$

$\frac{19}{6} =$

$\frac{35}{10} =$

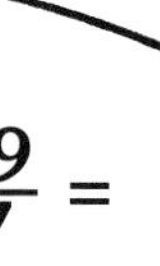

$\frac{27}{8} =$

$\frac{31}{9} =$

$\frac{17}{3} =$

$\frac{19}{7} =$

B Find the pairs of equivalent questions and join them to their answers.

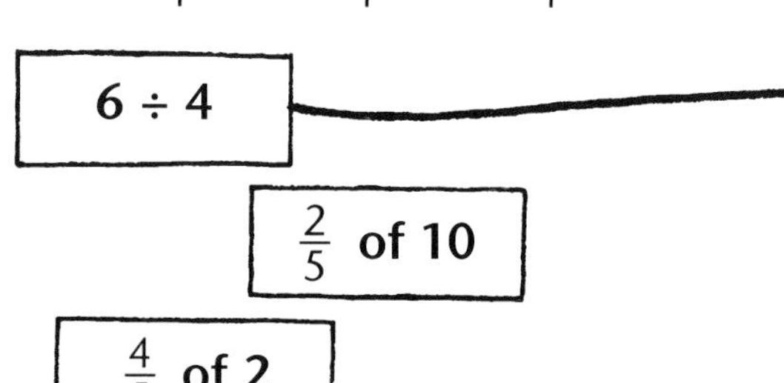

Questions	Answers	Questions
$6 \div 4$	$1\frac{1}{2}$	$6 \times \frac{1}{3}$
$\frac{2}{5}$ of 10	2	$3 \times \frac{3}{4}$
$\frac{4}{5}$ of 2	4	$6 \times \frac{1}{4}$
$\frac{1}{3}$ of 6	$2\frac{1}{4}$	$10 \div 5 \times 2$
$3 \div 4 \times 3$	$1\frac{3}{5}$	$2 \times \frac{4}{5}$

Remember that improper fractions are ones in which the numerator is larger than the denominator. They can be changed into **mixed numbers**, for example $\frac{13}{5} = 2\frac{3}{5}$. To do this, think how many of each part make up one whole (for example five-fifths). See how many lots of this you have to find the whole number part of the mixed number.

Fraction action

Multiply fractions by integers, including mixed numbers

When you multiply a fraction by an **integer**, you can think of this as several 'lots of' the fraction. So, $\frac{1}{2} \times 5$ can be thought of as '$\frac{1}{2}$ multiplied by 5' or '5 lots of $\frac{1}{2}$'.

Each of the straws below is one whole. Shade fractions of the straws to help you complete the multiplications.

(a) $\frac{1}{2} \times 5 = \frac{5}{2} = 2\frac{1}{2}$

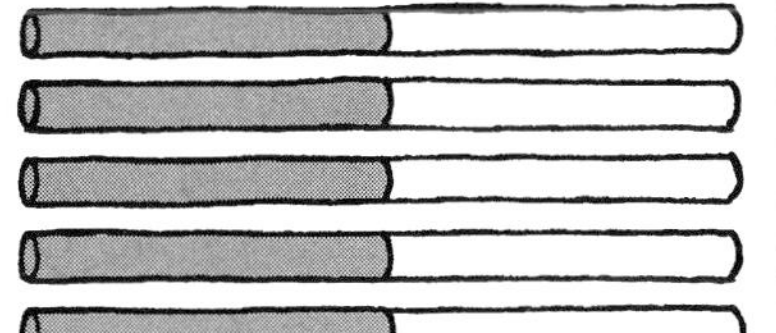

(b) $\frac{2}{3} \times 3 =$

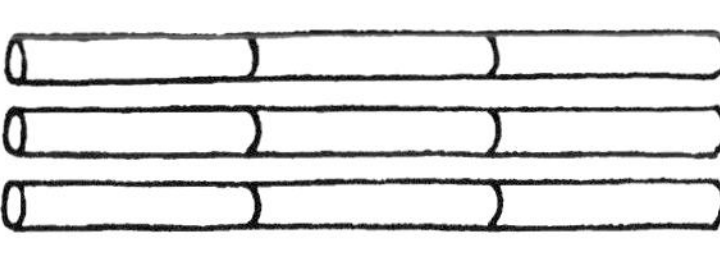

(c) $\frac{3}{4} \times 4 =$

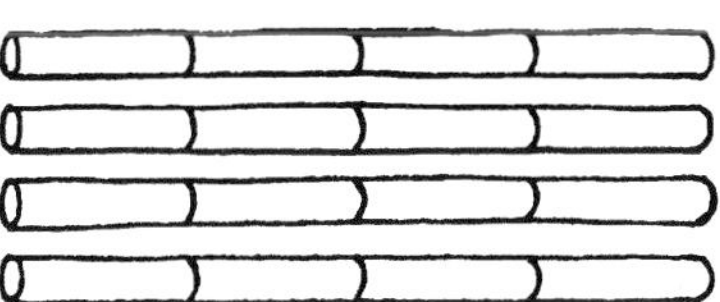

(d) $\frac{2}{3} \times 5 =$

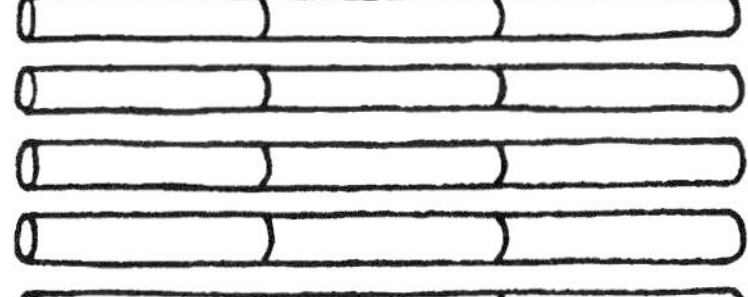

(e) $\frac{2}{5} \times 3 =$

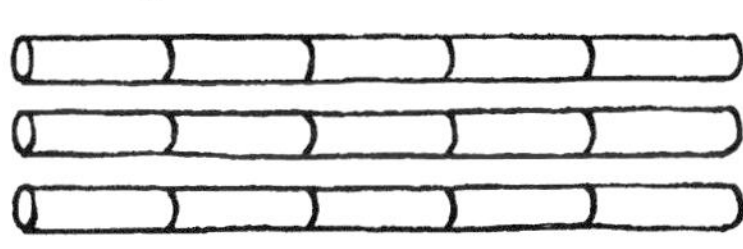

(f) $\frac{4}{5} \times 3 =$

(g) $\frac{3}{5} \times 2 =$

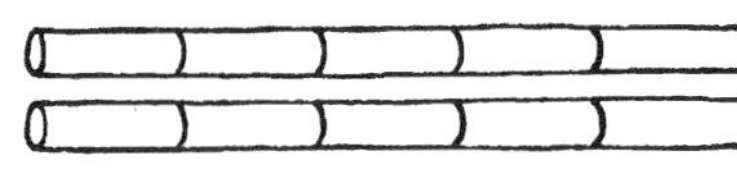

(h) $\frac{2}{5} \times 4 =$

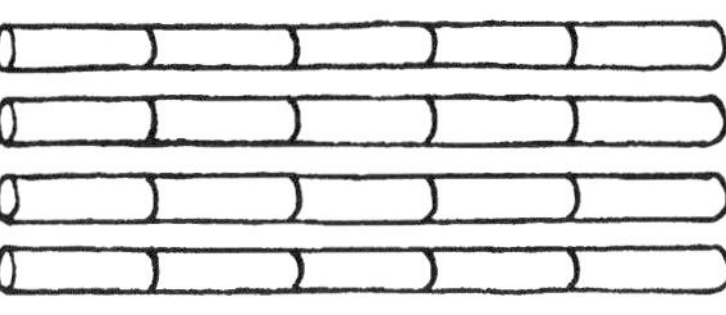

(i) $\frac{3}{8} \times 5 =$

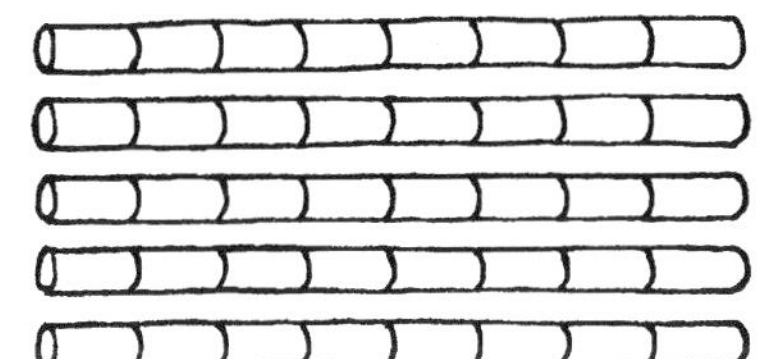

(j) $\frac{2}{3} \times 4 =$

(k) $\frac{4}{5} \times 2 =$

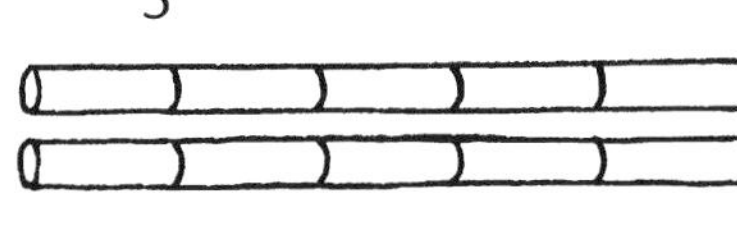

(l) $\frac{5}{8} \times 3 =$

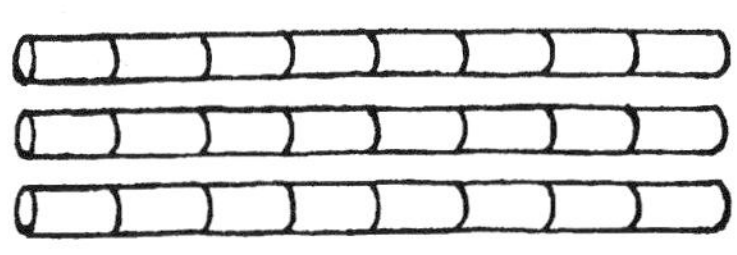

NOW TRY THIS!

- Which of the multiplications above have the same answer? List them in pairs.
- Write what you notice about the questions in each pair.

Remember that an **integer** is a positive or negative whole number. Convert the improper fractions in your answers to mixed numbers, for example $\frac{8}{5} = 1\frac{3}{5}$. To do this, think how many of each part make up one whole, for example five-fifths. See how many lots of this you have; this gives you the whole number part of the mixed number.

Find equivalent percentages, fractions and decimals

F-D-Ps

1. For a charity event, a sweet manufacturer has made a giant packet of sweets. Fill in the boxes to show the percentage, decimal and fraction equivalents of the packet. Give the fractions in their simplest form.

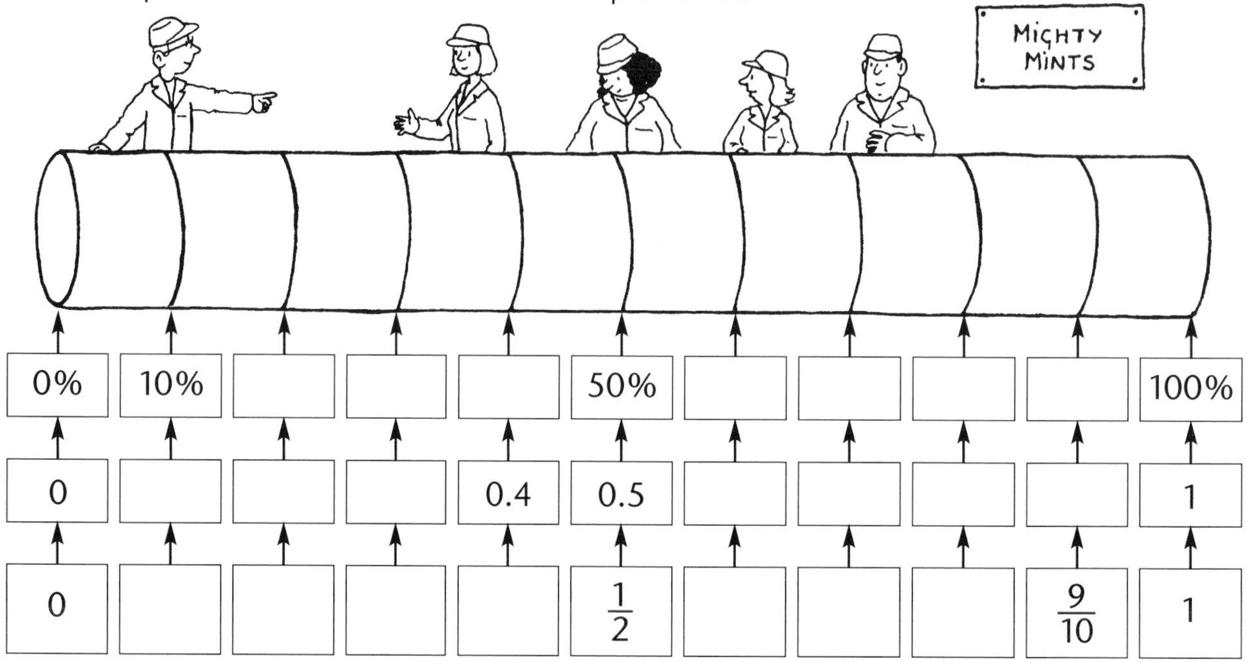

2. Mark the packet with a dotted line to show:
   (a) 25% **(b)** $\frac{3}{4}$ **(c)** 0.05 **(d)** 97%

3. Write which is the larger in each pair:

   (a) 25% or 0.3 ______ **(b)** $\frac{3}{4}$ or 0.7 ______ **(c)** 0.05 or 10% ______

   (d) 97% or $\frac{9}{10}$ ______ **(e)** $\frac{1}{5}$ or 10% ______ **(f)** $\frac{4}{5}$ or 75% ______

Use the diagram above to help you write the percentage, decimal and fraction equivalents. Give the fractions in their simplest form.

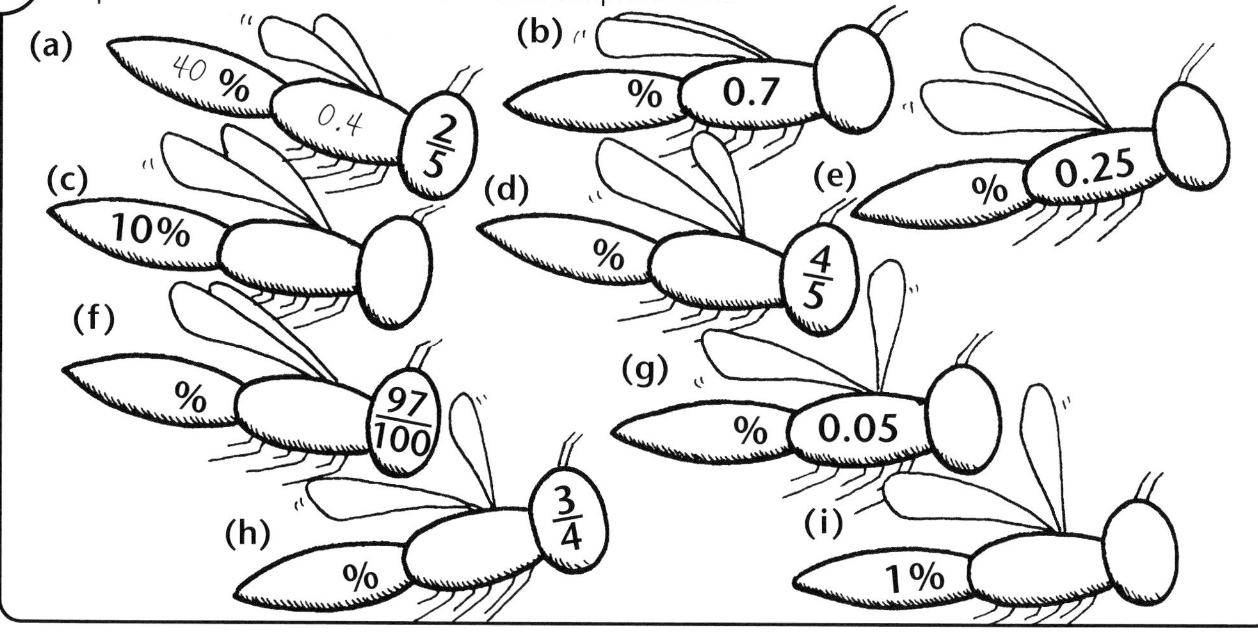

To change a fraction to its simplest form, divide the numerator (top number) and the denominator (bottom number) by the same whole number until there is no other number that will divide exactly into both: for example, $\frac{8}{10}$ is written as $\frac{4}{5}$ in its simplest form, as both numbers can be divided by 2.

F-D-Ps

Find equivalent percentages, fractions and decimals

1. Write the decimal and fraction equivalents of each percentage. Give the fractions in their simplest form.

(a) About 85% of the island of Greenland is white, not green!

0.85, $\frac{17}{20}$

(b) About 60% of the world's population lives in Asia.

(c) About 68% of the Earth's surface is covered with water.

(d) Only 12% of the volume of an iceberg is above water.

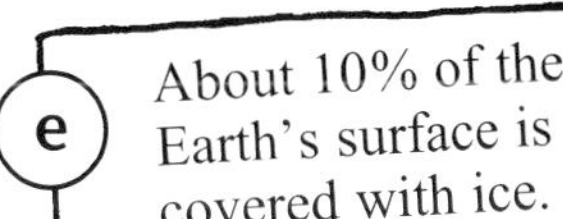

(e) About 10% of the Earth's surface is covered with ice.

(f) The Pacific Ocean covers about 32% of the Earth's surface.

(g) The oceans and seas account for 94% of water in the world.

(h) The Atlantic Ocean covers about 15% of the Earth's surface.

(i) About 19% of the Earth's surface is covered with deserts.

(j) About 5% of the water on Earth is fresh water, rather than salty water.

(k) Most oceans and seas are about 3% salt.

(l) The Red Sea is 4% salt.

2. Complete these facts. Give the fractions in their simplest form.

(a) 1% = $\frac{1}{100}$ = 0.01 (b) 2% = ____ = ____ (c) 6% = ____ = ____

(d) 17% = ____ = ____ (e) 35% = ____ = ____ (f) 96% = ____ = ____

NOW TRY THIS!

- Change these fractions and decimals to percentages. Then find the total of each row, diagonal and column.

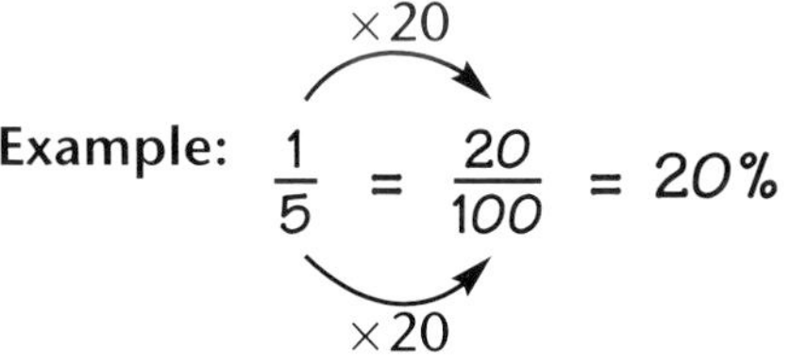

Example: $\frac{1}{5} = \frac{20}{100} = 20\%$ (×20)

$\frac{1}{5}$	0.3	$\frac{31}{100}$
0.06	$\frac{1}{4}$	0.2
$\frac{21}{50}$	0.5	$\frac{3}{20}$

To change a fraction to its simplest form, divide the numerator (top number) and the denominator (bottom number) by the same whole number until there is no other number that will divide exactly into both: for example, $\frac{60}{100}$ is written as $\frac{3}{5}$ in its simplest form, as both numbers can be divided by 20.

Calculate percentages mentally or using informal methods

Mental moments

1. Jack has drawn a diagram to show how he finds 75% of a number.

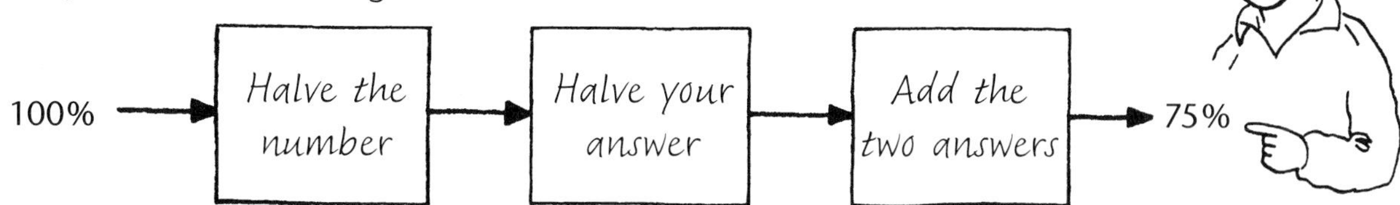

Check Jack's method by finding 75% of these numbers.

(a) 48 ______	**(b)** 12 ______	**(c)** 56 ______	**(d)** 120 ______
(e) 84 ______	**(f)** 200 ______	**(g)** 144 ______	**(h)** 10 ______

2. Molly has drawn a diagram to show how she finds 15% of a number.

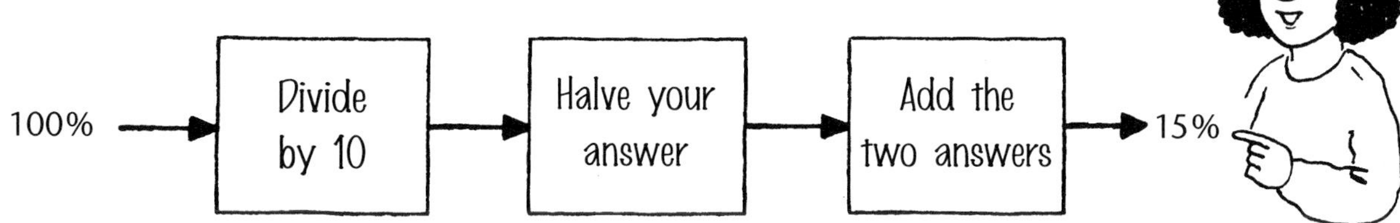

Check Molly's method by finding 15% of these numbers.

(a) 40 ______	**(b)** 60 ______	**(c)** 700 ______	**(d)** 120 ______
(e) 300 ______	**(f)** 150 ______	**(g)** 90 ______	**(h)** 14 ______

B

1. Complete these diagrams to show how to find 60%, 11%, 9% and 99% of a number. Use as many boxes as you wish. If you need more, draw the diagram on the back of this sheet.

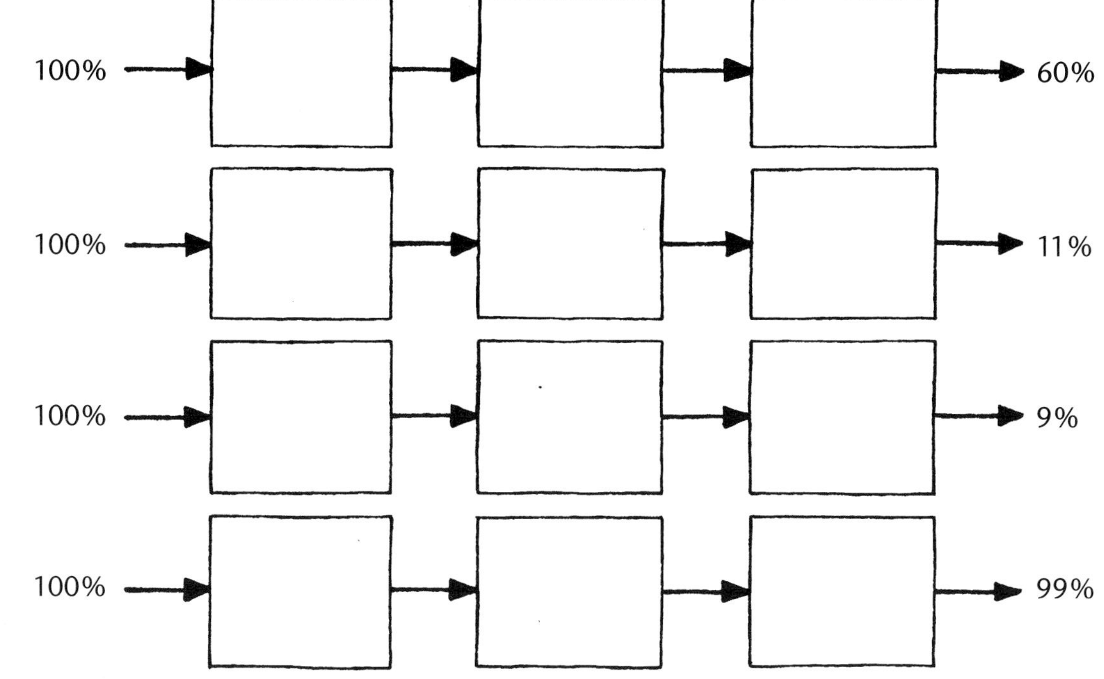

2. Test your diagrams by finding these percentages of the numbers 600 and 120.

There are many different ways of finding percentages of numbers in your head: for example, 75% can also be found by finding 25% (one quarter) and subtracting it from 100%.

Mental moments

Calculate percentages mentally or using informal methods

C Play this game with a partner.

- ☆ Take turns to choose a percentage from the parasol and a number from the rug.
- ☆ Work out the percentage of the number.
- ☆ If the answer is between 50 and 100 you score a point.
- ☆ Record every question and answer to make sure no question is repeated.
- ☆ The winner is the first player to score 16 points.

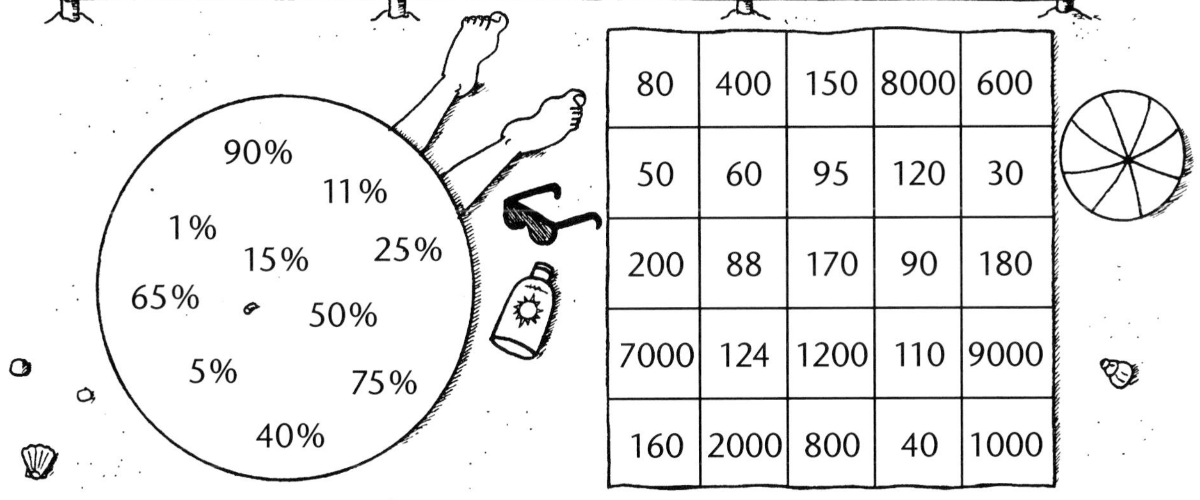

80	400	150	8000	600
50	60	95	120	30
200	88	170	90	180
7000	124	1200	110	9000
160	2000	800	40	1000

Our questions and answers

- Write the number 80 in the middle of a sheet of paper.
- Find at least 20 different percentages of this number.

Example:

50% of 80 = 40

80

5% of 80 = …

15% of 80 = …

When you are finding percentages, you may sometimes get an answer that is not a whole number, for example 1% of 80 = 80 divided by 100 = 0.8.

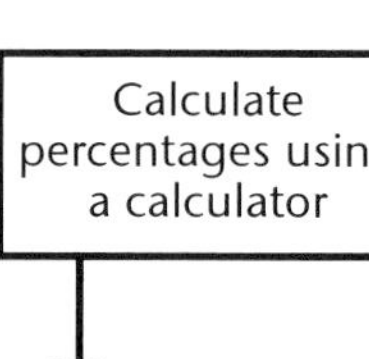

Calculator calculations

A Sally is explaining how she used a calculator to work out this percentage.

Sally's Silly Sale!

I changed 37% to a fraction by writing it as an amount 'out of 100': $\frac{37}{100} = 37 \div 100$.

To find 37% of 4800 I keyed in '37 ÷ 100 × 4800 =' and got the answer 1776.
So, 37% of £4800 is **£1776**.

Use Sally's method to find these sale prices with a calculator.

(a) 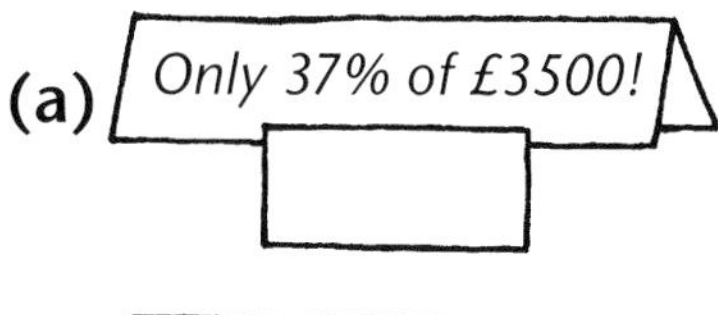

(b) 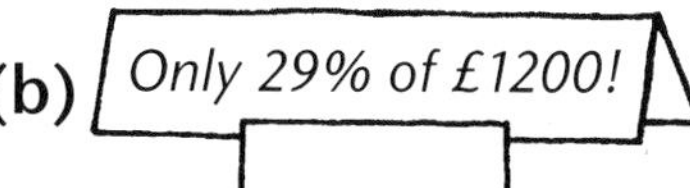

(c) 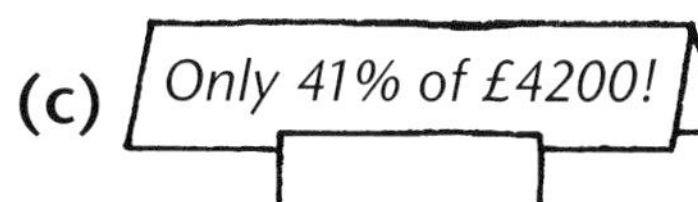

(d) 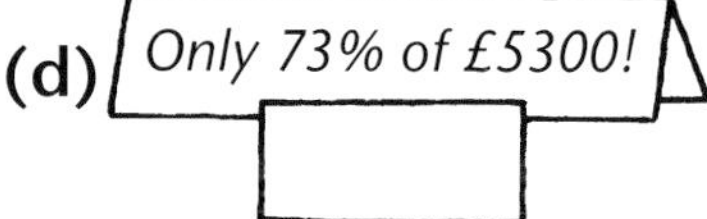

(e) 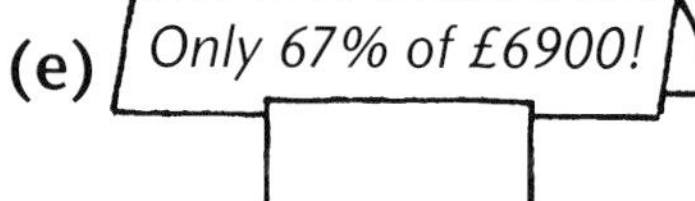

(f) 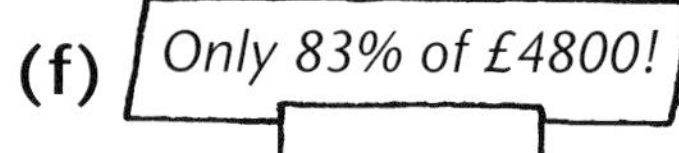

(g) 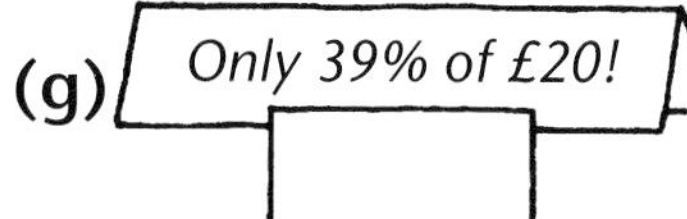

(h) 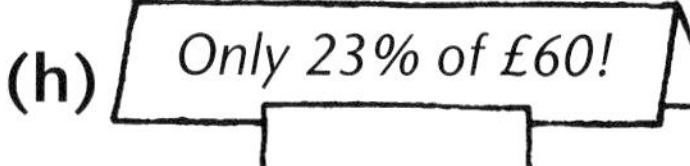

(i) 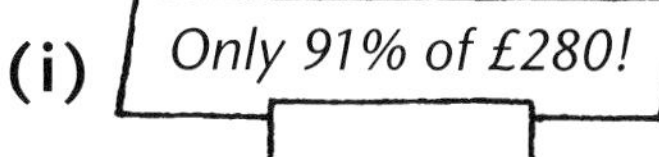

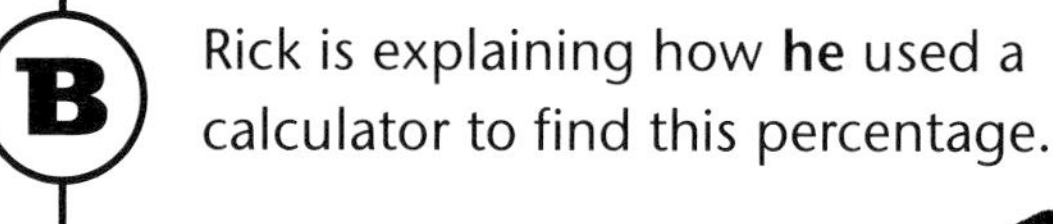

B Rick is explaining how **he** used a calculator to find this percentage.

I changed 45% to the decimal 0.45 in my head.
To find 45% of 42 I keyed in '0.45 × 42 =' and got the answer 18.9.
So, 45% of £42 is **£18.90**.

Use Rick's method to find these sale prices with a calculator.

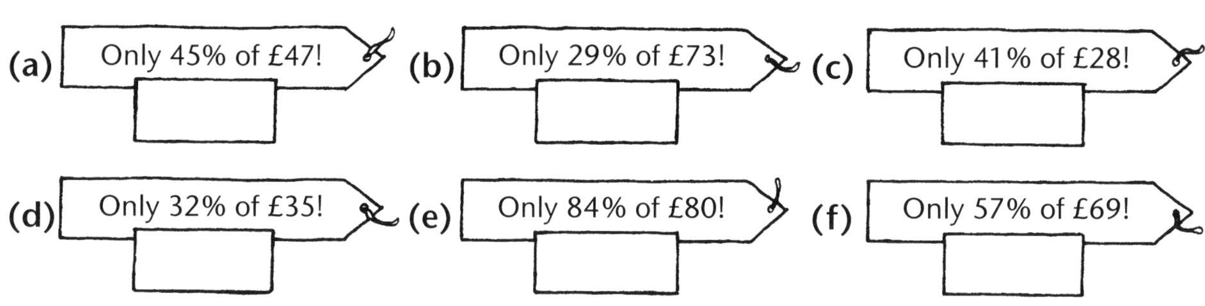

Did you find Sally's or Rick's method quicker? __________

Why? __________

Try to get into the habit of placing the calculator on the table and using your non-writing hand to key in the numbers. This allows you to write things down as you use the calculator and will save you time in the future. With money questions, remember to write your answers in pounds and pence instead of ordinary decimals, for example £23.40 not 23.4.

Calculator calculations

Calculate percentages using a calculator

This catalogue page shows the price list of a shop called 'Hikeaway'.

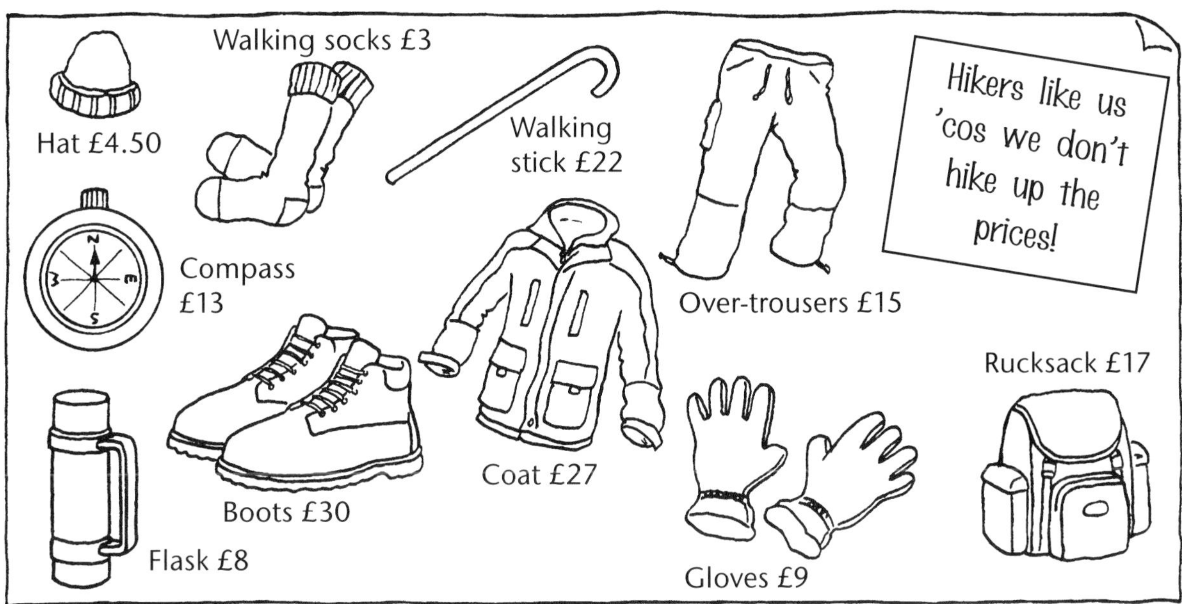

In the sale, each item is sold for a percentage of its catalogue price.

1. Work out the sale prices of these items. **Sale price**

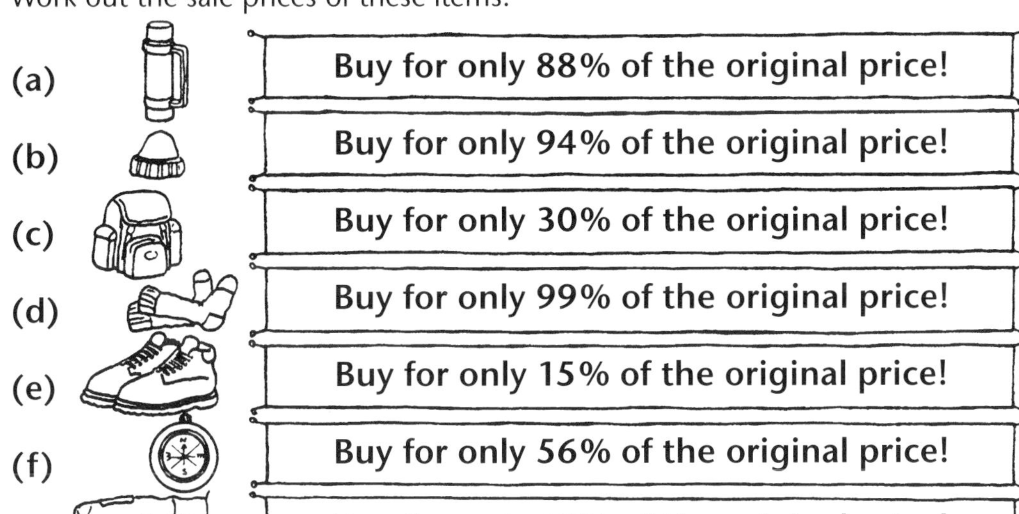

		Sale price
(a)	Buy for only 88% of the original price!	
(b)	Buy for only 94% of the original price!	
(c)	Buy for only 30% of the original price!	
(d)	Buy for only 99% of the original price!	
(e)	Buy for only 15% of the original price!	
(f)	Buy for only 56% of the original price!	
(g)	Buy for only 47% of the original price!	
(h)	Buy for only 25% of the original price!	

2. Which item has the greatest reduction in price? ______

NOW TRY THIS!

- Work out the original prices of these items.

Original price		Sale price
	Buy for only 77% of the original price!	£15.40
	Buy for only 84% of the original price!	£7.56

With money questions, remember to write your answers in pounds and pence instead of as ordinary decimals, for example £8.40 rather than 8.4.

Use percentages to compare simple proportions

Percentage proportions

1. Look at the clothing labels. What proportion of each garment is cotton?

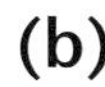

(a)

POLYESTER	74%
ELASTANE	2%
COTTON	24 %

(b)

SILK	42%
COTTON	____%
NYLON	12%

(c)

NYLON	48%
WOOL	17%
COTTON	____%
SILK	4%

(d)

ACRYLIC	19%
ELASTANE	6%
COTTON	____%

(e)

COTTON	____%
SILK	12%
NYLON	16%
POLYESTER	32%

(f)

VISCOSE	79%
COTTON	____%
POLYESTER	4%
ELASTANE	3%

(g)

POLYESTER	88%
ELASTANE	2%
NYLON	4%
COTTON	____%

(h)

SILK	63%
COTTON	____%
NYLON	22%
ELASTANE	4%

2. Look at these 10 tops.

What proportion of them have:

(a) spots? ____ % (b) a slogan? ____ % (c) long sleeves? ____ %

Here are 40 pupils.

What proportion:

(a) are female? ____ % (b) have glasses? ____ %

(c) are wearing skirts? ____ % (d) are wearing trousers? ____ %

(e) have hats? ____ % (f) are wearing ties? ____ %

Proportion compares one part with the whole, for example black hats out of the total number of hats. Proportions can be written as fractions, decimals or percentages. In part B, first write the proportion as a fraction in its simplest form, and then think what percentage is equivalent to this fraction, for example $\frac{4}{40} = \frac{1}{10}$ = 10%.

Percentage proportions

Use percentages to compare simple proportions

1. The grey strip on each battery shows how much power is left. Estimate the **proportion** of the battery power that is left.

(a)  30 %

(b)  ____ %

(c) 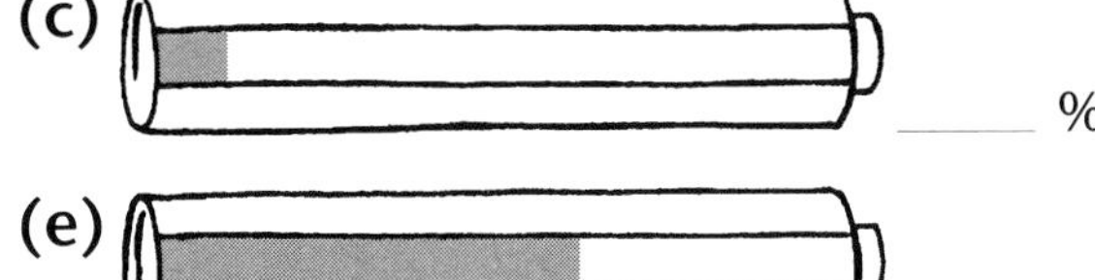 ____ %

(d) 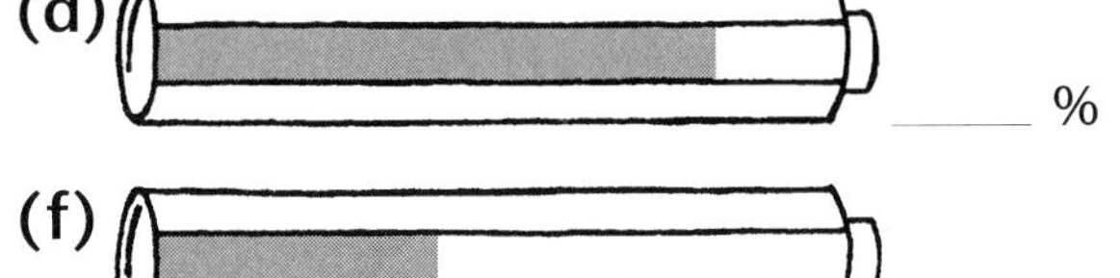 ____ %

(e) ____ %

(f) ____ %

2. Colour each section of the pie chart in a different colour. Estimate the percentage of the chart that each colour represents and fill in the key.

(a)

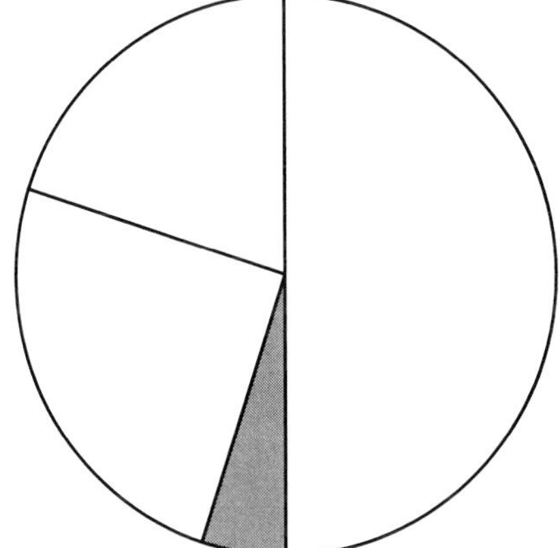

Colour key	Approximate percentage
grey	5%

(b)

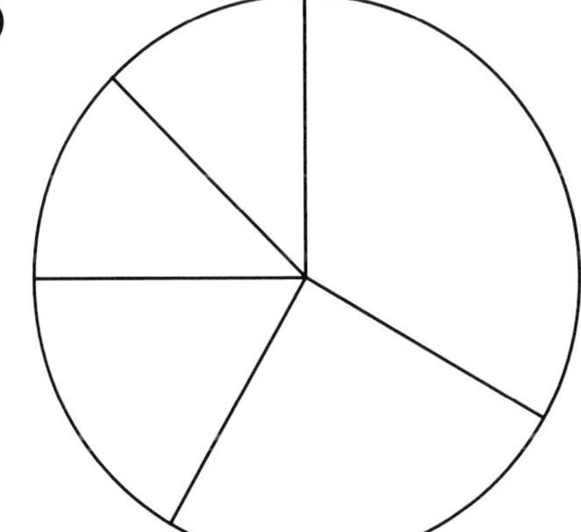

Colour key	Approximate percentage

NOW TRY THIS!

64% of the pupils in Year 7 are girls. 25% of the girls and 50% of the boys own a portable CD player. What proportion of Year 7 owns a portable CD player? ____ %

Proportion compares one part with the whole, for example black hats out of the total number of hats. Proportions can be written as fractions, decimals or percentages. In question 2, remember that your estimates should have a total of 100%.

Use direct proportion in simple contexts

It's all Greek to me!

A

1. The recipes in this Greek cookbook show the ingredients needed for five people.

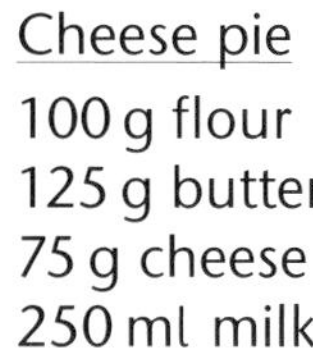

Cheese pie
100 g flour
125 g butter
75 g cheese
250 ml milk

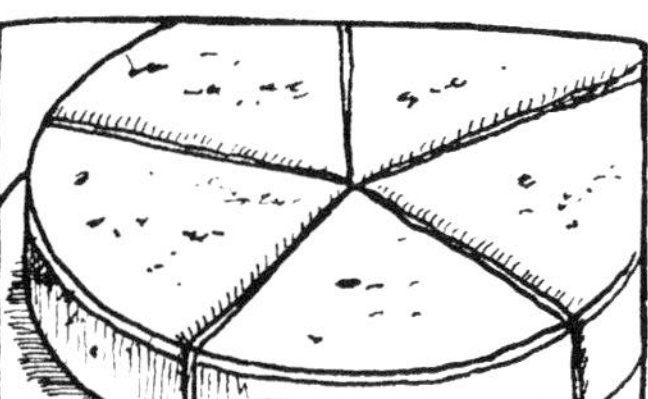

Spinach parcels
205 g flour
5 eggs
150 ml water
195 g spinach

Sweet pastries
210 g sugar
175 g flour
15 g jam
5 eggs

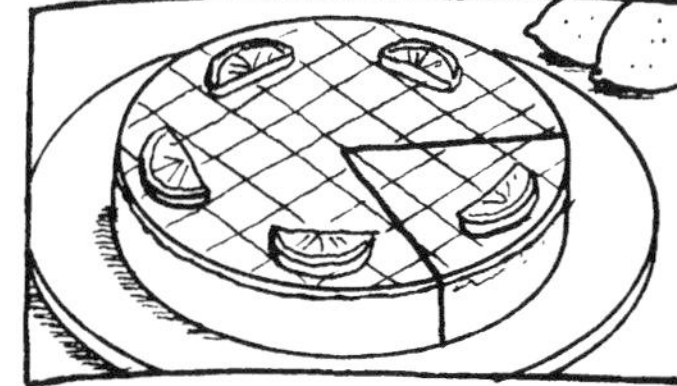

Lemon cake
$2\frac{1}{2}$ lemons
225 g sugar
230 g flour
130 g butter

Rewrite each recipe to show the ingredients needed for two people.

Cheese pie	Sweet pastries	Spinach parcels	Lemon cake
40 g flour	____ g sugar	____ g flour	____ lemons
____ g butter	____ g flour	____ eggs	____ g sugar
____ g cheese	____ g jam	____ ml water	____ g flour
____ ml milk	____ eggs	____ g spinach	____ g butter

2. On holiday, Chris changes some pounds into euros. The bank gives 1.25 euros for every pound. How many euros does Chris get if he changes:

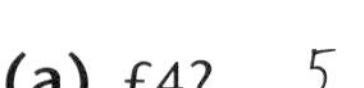

(a) £4? 5 **(b)** £8? ____

(c) £12? ____ **(d)** £16? ____

(e) £20? ____ **(f)** £24? ____

(g) £28? ____ **(h)** £32? ____

B Work out the equivalent amounts in euros.

(a) £10 = 10 x 1.25 = 12.5 euros **(b)** £5 = ____

(c) £3 = ____ **(d)** £7 = ____

(e) £9 = ____ **(f)** £11 = ____

With questions of this type, it is helpful to work out what 'one' of something is worth, for example what £1 is worth or how much of an ingredient is needed for one person.

It's all Greek to me!

Use direct proportion in simple contexts

1. Look at the Greek restaurant's price list. The prices are in euros.

Lamb kebabs	€4.45
Squid rings	€2.00
Greek salad	€2.36
Grilled fish	€3.95
Stuffed peppers	€2.95
Tomato salad	€1.75
Spinach parcels	€3.55

(a) Two people choose the same dish. They pay €8.90 in total. Which dish did they choose?

____

(b) What would be the total cost if three people chose this dish?

____

(c) A family of four all choose the same dish. They pay €8 in total. What would they pay if there were only three of them eating this dish?

____

(d) A family of five all choose the same dish. They pay €11.80 in total. What would they pay if there were only three of them eating this dish?

____

(e) A family of four all choose the same dish. They pay €15.80 in total. What would they pay if there were only three of them eating this dish?

____

(f) Two people choose the same dish. They pay €3.50 in total. What would be the total cost if three people chose this dish?

____

(g) A family of five all choose the same dish. They pay €17.75 in total. What would they pay if there were only three of them eating this dish?

____

(h) Six people choose the same dish. They pay €17.70 in total. What would they pay if there were only five of them eating this dish?

____

(i) Two people choose the same dish. They pay €7.10 in total. What would be the total cost if seven people chose this dish?

____

2. Is it possible to answer all the questions above without looking at the price list? ______

NOW TRY THIS!

This is a rule for changing pounds into euros.

Multiply the number of pounds by 1.25

- Write the opposite rule for changing euros into pounds.
- Use your rule to convert the price list above into pounds.

In C1, find out what one person's dish costs by dividing, and then multiply to find how much it would cost for more than one person. To change euros into pounds, you need to do the opposite of multiplying by 1.25.

Understand ratio and proportion

Beady-eyed

Shade each row of beads to match the statement.

Proportion

(a) The proportion of grey beads is 10%.

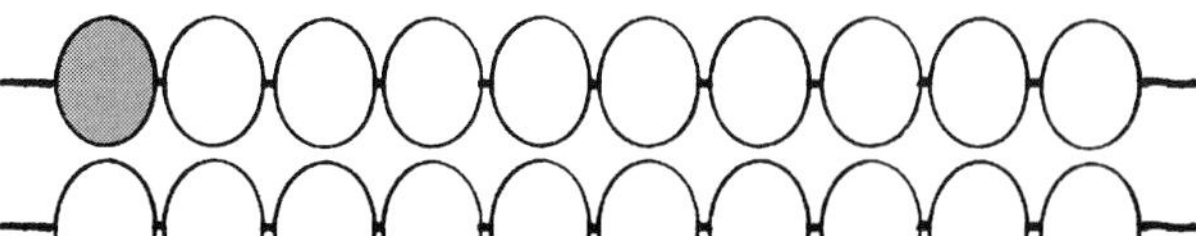

(b) The proportion of white beads is 0.5.

(c) The proportion of grey beads is $\frac{1}{5}$.

(d) The proportion of white beads is 70%.

(e) The proportion of grey beads is 100%.

Ratio

(f) The ratio of grey to white beads is one part to nine parts, or 1 : 9.

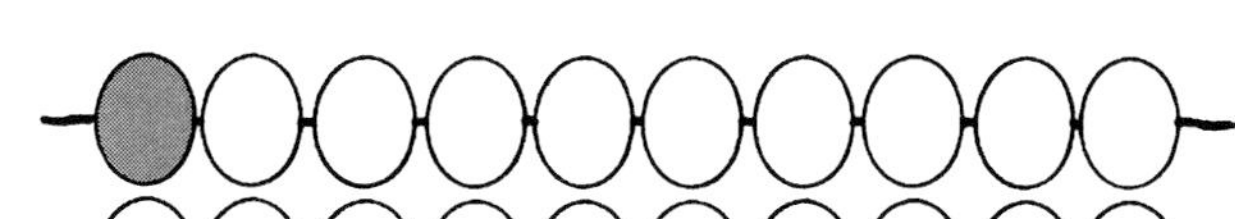

(g) The ratio of grey to white beads is 7 : 3.

(h) The ratio of grey to white beads is 1 : 4.

(i) The ratio of grey to white beads is 2 : 3.

(j) The ratio of grey to white beads is 4 : 1.

(k) The ratio of grey to white beads is 3 : 2.

1. Complete these statements for this row of beads.

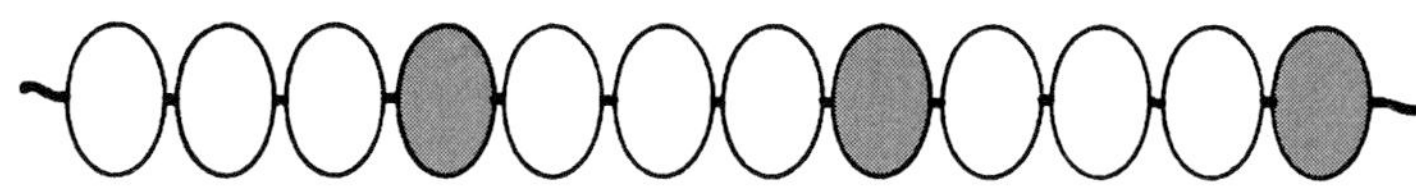

(a) The ratio of white to grey beads is ________.

(b) The ratio of grey to white beads is ________.

(c) The proportion of white beads as a fraction of the total is ________.

(d) The proportion of grey beads as a fraction of the total is ________.

(e) The proportion of grey beads is ________%.

(f) The proportion of white beads is ________%.

2. On a separate piece of paper, write at least four true statements about this row of beads.

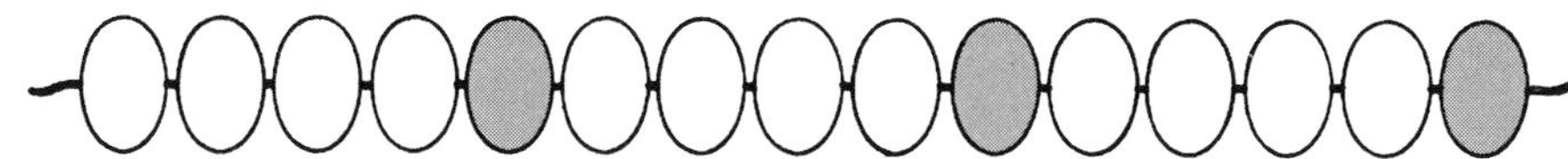

Ratio compares one part with another part, for example comparing white beads with grey beads. **Proportion** compares one part with the whole, for example grey beads out of the total number of beads. Proportions can be written as fractions, decimals or percentages.

Beady-eyed

Understand ratio and proportion

1. Give the **proportion** of black beads in each jar as a fraction, decimal and percentage. Write the fractions in their simplest form.

(a) 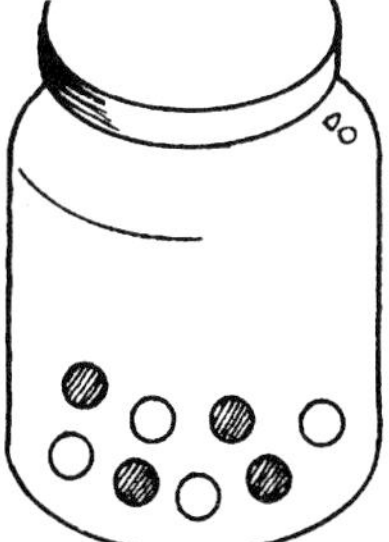

Fraction $\frac{1}{2}$
Decimal 0.5
Percentage 50%

(b) 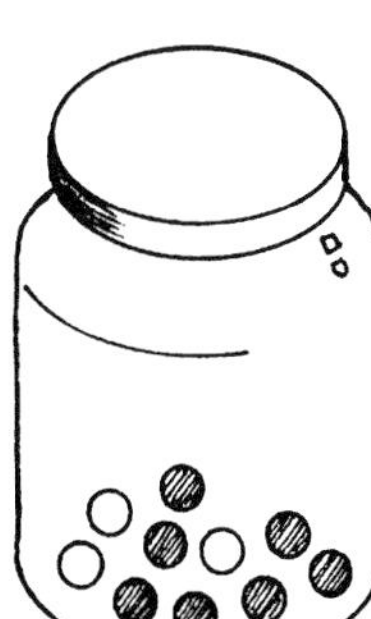

Fraction ______
Decimal ______
Percentage ______

(c) 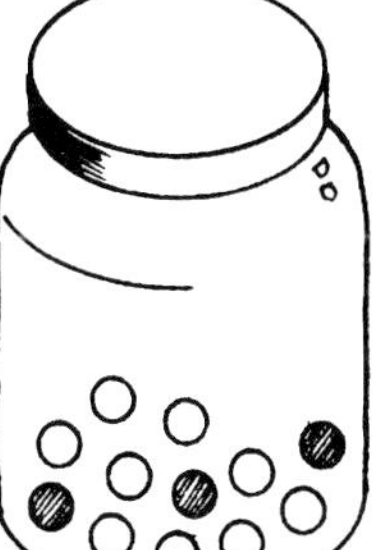

Fraction ______
Decimal ______
Percentage ______

(d) 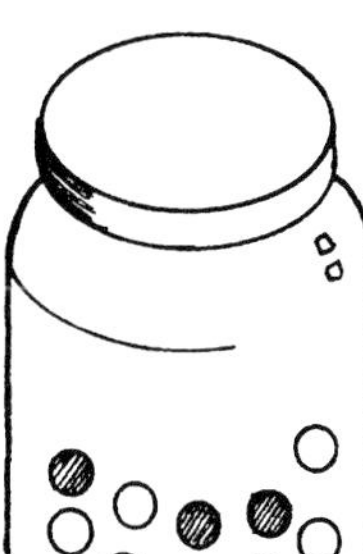

Fraction ______
Decimal ______
Percentage ______

(e) 

Fraction ______
Decimal ______
Percentage ______

(f) 

Fraction ______
Decimal ______
Percentage ______

(g) 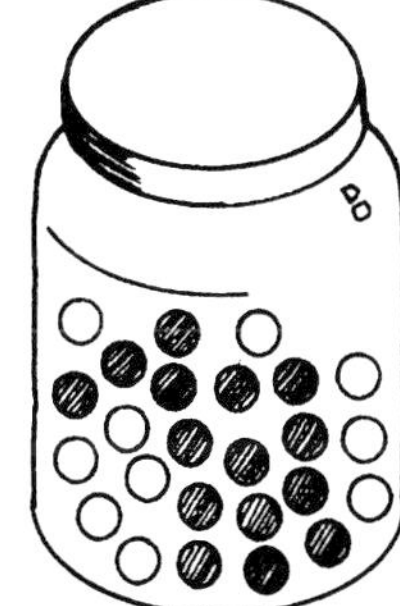

Fraction ______
Decimal ______
Percentage ______

(h) 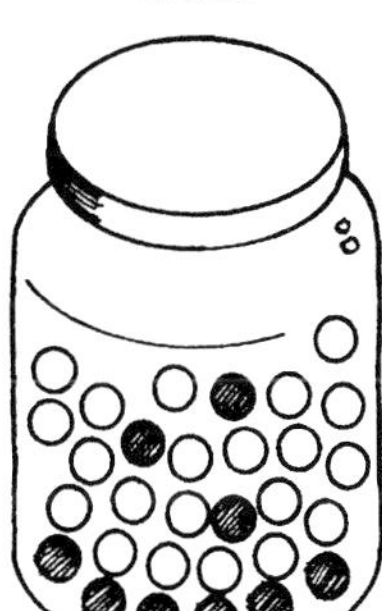

Fraction ______
Decimal ______
Percentage ______

2. Now write the **ratio**, in its simplest form, of black to white beads in each jar.

(a) 1 : 1 (b) ______ (c) ______ (d) ______
(e) ______ (f) ______ (g) ______ (h) ______

NOW TRY THIS!

In a safari park there are 5 lions, 25 gazelles and 30 monkeys.

(a) What is the proportion of lions? ______
(b) What is the ratio of lions to gazelles? ______
(c) What is the ratio of gazelles to monkeys? ______

Ratio compares one part with another part, for example comparing white beads with black beads. **Proportion** compares one part with the whole, for example black beads out of the total number of beads. Proportions can be written as fractions, decimals or percentages.

Solve simple ratio problems using informal strategies

Problems with ratios!

A Eight groups of pupils are going on a school trip. Each group has a different ratio of males to females.

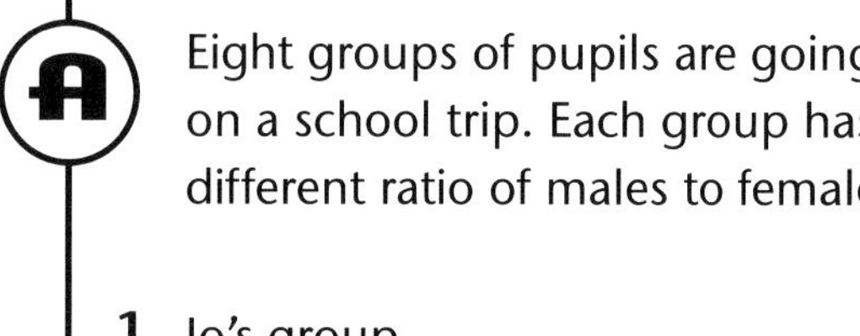

1. Jo's group
There is **1** male for every **3** females.
There are **7** males in the group.
How many females are there? ☐

M : F
×7 (1 : 3) ×7
7 : ?

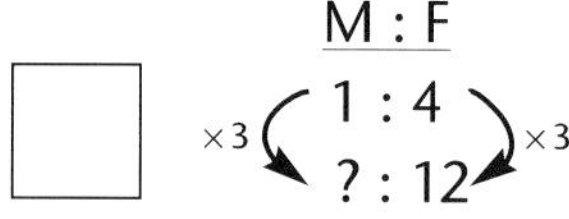

2. Rob's group
There is **1** male for every **4** females.
There are **12** females in the group.
How many males are there? ☐

M : F
×3 (1 : 4) ×3
? : 12

3. Raz's group
There are **3** males for every **2** females.
There are **12** males in the group.
How many females are there? ☐

M : F
(3 : 2)
:

4. Deepa's group
There are **5** males for every **7** females.
There are **28** females in the group.
How many males are there? ☐

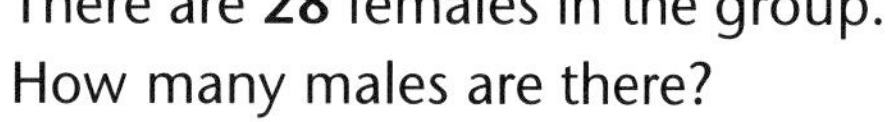

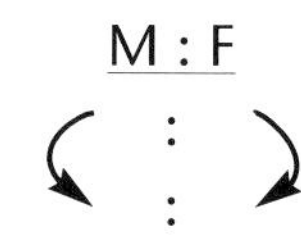

M : F
(:)
:

B

1. Clive's group
There are **5** males for every **3** females.
There are **24 people** in total.
How many males and how many females are there?

males ☐ females ☐

M : F
×3 (5 : 3 → 8) ×3
? : ? → 24

2. Sam's group
There are **2** males for every **5** females.
There are **35 people** in total.
How many males and how many females are there?

males ☐ females ☐

M : F
(2 : 5 → 7)
: →

3. Davina's group
There is **1** male for every **2** females.
There are **24 people** in total.
How many males and how many females are there?

males ☐ females ☐

M : F
(: →)
: →

4. Sanjay's group
There are **4** males for every **7** females.
There are **55 people** in total.
How many males and how many females are there?

males ☐ females ☐

M : F
(: →)
: →

You can multiply or divide the numbers in a ratio by any number, and as long as you do the same to **all** the numbers the relationship will still be the same. Record the ratio, find what to multiply the numbers by, and then use this to find the answer.

Problems with ratios!

Solve simple ratio problems using informal strategies

1. This week's chart shows Kandystix outselling Rosie Reid in the ratio 3 : 2. Kandystix sold 3000 singles. How many did Rosie Reid sell? [ ]

2. So far this season United have scored 4 goals for every 3 goals City have scored. City have scored 27 goals. How many have United scored? [ ]

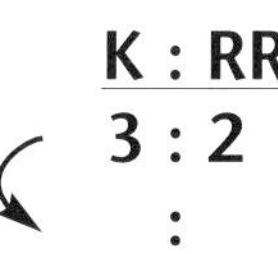

K : RR
3 : 2
:

U : C
:
:

3. Big Burgers sell 4 cheeseburgers for every 9 hamburgers. Yesterday they sold 39 burgers. How many of each type did they sell?

c/burger	h/burger

4. Dave and Judy win £14 000 and agree to share the money in the ratio 3 : 4. How much does each get?

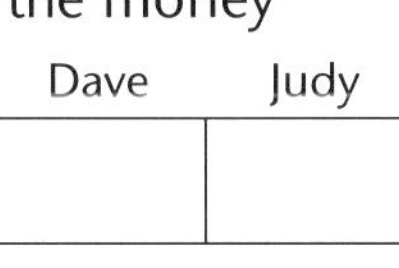

Dave	Judy

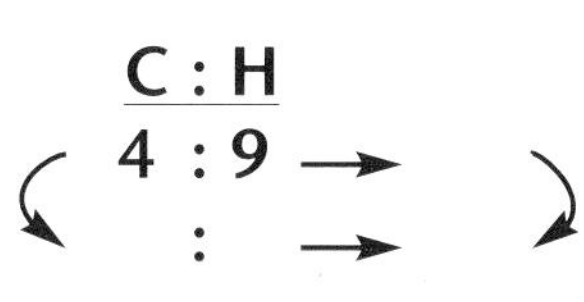

C : H
4 : 9 →
: →

D : J
3 : 4 →
: →

5. McMickey's sell 2 strawberry milkshakes for every 5 chocolate milkshakes. On Monday they sold 40 chocolate ones. How many strawberry milkshakes did they sell? [ ]

6. A cement mix is made using 3 parts cement and 5 parts sand. Simon makes a 24 kg mix. How much sand and cement does he use?

sand	cement

NOW TRY THIS!

(a) Andy, Mandy and Sandy share £45 in the ratio 4 : 3 : 2.

How much does each person get?

Andy	Mandy	Sandy

(b) The Paint Shop mixes purple paint using 3 parts white, 2 parts blue and 1 part red.

It makes 30 litres of purple paint.

How much of each colour is used?

white	blue	red

(c) In a sponsored walk, Zoë, Chloë and Joey raise a total of £175 in the ratio 6 : 11 : 8.

How much does each person raise?

Zoë	Chloë	Joey

You can multiply or divide the numbers in a ratio by any number, and as long as you do the same to **all** the numbers, the relationship will still be the same. Record the ratio, find what to multiply the numbers by, and then use this to find the answer.

Answers

p 8

A2 (a) 800 (b) 50 (c) 2000
(d) 70 000 (e) 800 000 (f) 9 000 000

A3 (a) 4 (b) 400 (c) 40
(d) 400 000 (e) 40 000 (f) 4000

p 9

C1 (a) 54 321 (b) 65 432 (c) 76 543
The digits in the original number are reversed.

C2 (a) 654 321 (b) 765 432 (c) 876 543
The digits in the original number are reversed.

C3 Six million, four hundred and nineteen thousand, seven hundred and fifty-four

C4 Seventy-five million, three hundred and eight thousand, six hundred and forty-three

p 10

A2 (a) $\frac{5}{100}$ (b) 40 (c) 200 000 (d) $\frac{1}{1000}$
(e) 9000 (f) 5 000 000 (g) $\frac{2}{10}$

A3 (a) 3000 (b) 3 (c) 30 000 (d) 300
(e) 300 000 (f) $\frac{3}{10}$ (g) $\frac{3}{1000}$

B (a) 3.6 3.7 3.8 3.9 4.0 4.1 4.2
(b) 4.05 4.06 4.07 4.08 4.09 4.10 4.11
(c) 8.3 8.2 8.1 8.0 7.9 7.8 7.7
(d) 0.32 0.31 0.30 0.29 0.28 0.27 0.26
(e) Add 0.11: 5.67 5.78 5.89 6.0 6.11 6.22 6.33
(f) Subtract 0.09: 9.32 9.23 9.14 9.05 8.96 8.87 8.78

p 11

C1 0.1 0.01 2 0.001 0.4 0.07 3 0.05 0.1 0.04
0.002 0.001 0.05 0.7 0.25

C2 (a) 6.476 (b) 6.807
(c) 3.807 (d) 4.566
(e) 3.857 (f) 4.466
(g) 3.807

C3 (a) 0.1 (b) 0.01
(c) 0.001 (d) 0.04
(e) 3 (f) 0.001

p 12

A1 (a) 5740 (e) 405 800
(b) 82 900 (f) 6 800 000
(c) 2 050 000 (g) 385 040
(d) 990 900 (h) 1 069 000

A2 (a) 4203 (e) 2058
(b) 1270 (f) 9144
(c) 608 (g) 624 504
(d) 59 199 (h) 2019

B (a) × 10
(b) ÷ 100
(c) × 100 (f) × 1000
(d) ÷ 100 (g) ÷ 10
(e) × 1000 (h) ÷ 10

p 13

C1 £1 90 p 50 p £1.80 £1.20

C2 (a) £992 (b) £323
£8928 £31 977
(c) £1549 (d) £58
£13 941 £57 942
(e) £116 (f) £102
£11 484 £101 898

p 14

A1 (a) 38 (e) 202.3
(b) 410 (f) 82 100
(c) 43 970 (g) 7620.6
(d) 8609 (h) 10 450

A2 (a) 5.7 (e) 30.58
(b) 8.22 (f) 5.4
(c) 5.06 (g) 411.04
(d) 194.52 (h) 20.29

B 3 670 000 2 450 000
367 000 245 000
36 700 24 500
3670 2450
367 245
36.7 24.5
3.67 2.45

p 15

C1 480 cm 925 cm
703 cm 690 cm
360 cm 67 cm
1.75 m 0.95 m
6.13 m 0.7 m
0.03 m 0.12 m
550 cm 680 cm
4675 g 567 g
6530 g 4700 g
6.3 kg 0.469 kg

C2 10

p 16

B (a) 0.31 m, 2.04 m, 2.13 m, 2.4 m
(b) 0.6 l, 0.66 l, 6.06 l, 6.6 l
(c) 5.04 km, 5.13 km, 5.31 km, 5.4 km
(d) 1.829 kg, 1.892 kg, 1.9 kg, 1.982 kg
(e) 0.018 m, 0.08 m, 0.081 m, 0.1 m

p 17

C1 (a) Football
(b) Volleyball
(c) Lacrosse

C2 0.018 km, 91.4 m, 100 m, 0.12 km

C3 (a) Table tennis
(b) Hockey
(c) Table tennis

C4 22.2 cm, 21.3 cm, 7.3 cm, 6.67 cm, 6.5 cm, 5.2 cm, 4.15 cm, 3.8 cm

p 18

A (a) £97 541
£76 211
£88 532
£96 422
£96 552
£98 700

(b) £98 700, £97 541, £96 552, £96 422, £88 532, £76 211

(c)

98 700	98 700	98 700	99 000
97 541	97 540	97 500	98 000
96 552	96 550	96 600	97 000
96 422	96 420	96 400	96 000
88 532	88 530	88 500	89 000
76 211	76 210	76 200	76 000

B1

98 529	→	99 000	98 699	→	99 000
97 489	→	97 000	98 480	→	98 000
99 501	→	100 000	96 500	→	97 000
99 499	→	99 000	97 541	→	98 000
99 517	→	100 000	100 388	→	100 000
100 741	→	101 000	99 801	→	100 000

B2 Lowest 97 500 Highest 98 499

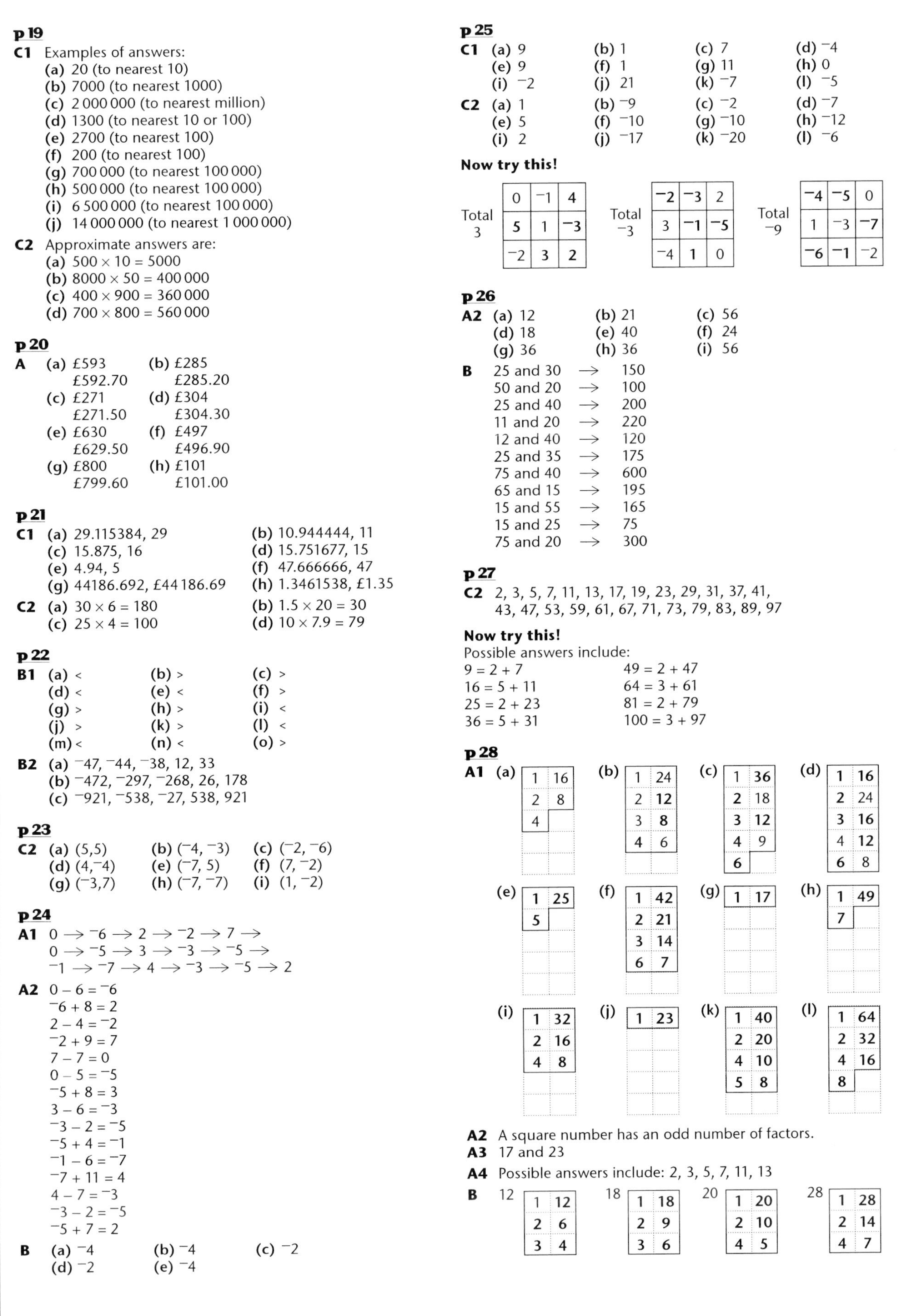

p 19

C1 Examples of answers:
(a) 20 (to nearest 10)
(b) 7000 (to nearest 1000)
(c) 2 000 000 (to nearest million)
(d) 1300 (to nearest 10 or 100)
(e) 2700 (to nearest 100)
(f) 200 (to nearest 100)
(g) 700 000 (to nearest 100 000)
(h) 500 000 (to nearest 100 000)
(i) 6 500 000 (to nearest 100 000)
(j) 14 000 000 (to nearest 1 000 000)

C2 Approximate answers are:
(a) $500 \times 10 = 5000$
(b) $8000 \times 50 = 400\,000$
(c) $400 \times 900 = 360\,000$
(d) $700 \times 800 = 560\,000$

p 20

A
(a) £593 £592.70
(b) £285 £285.20
(c) £271 £271.50
(d) £304 £304.30
(e) £630 £629.50
(f) £497 £496.90
(g) £800 £799.60
(h) £101 £101.00

p 21

C1
(a) 29.115384, 29
(b) 10.944444, 11
(c) 15.875, 16
(d) 15.751677, 15
(e) 4.94, 5
(f) 47.666666, 47
(g) 44186.692, £44 186.69
(h) 1.3461538, £1.35

C2
(a) $30 \times 6 = 180$
(b) $1.5 \times 20 = 30$
(c) $25 \times 4 = 100$
(d) $10 \times 7.9 = 79$

p 22

B1
(a) < (b) > (c) >
(d) < (e) < (f) >
(g) > (h) > (i) <
(j) > (k) > (l) <
(m) < (n) < (o) >

B2
(a) $^{-}47, {}^{-}44, {}^{-}38, 12, 33$
(b) $^{-}472, {}^{-}297, {}^{-}268, 26, 178$
(c) $^{-}921, {}^{-}538, {}^{-}27, 538, 921$

p 23

C2
(a) (5,5) (b) $(^{-}4, {}^{-}3)$ (c) $(^{-}2, {}^{-}6)$
(d) $(4, {}^{-}4)$ (e) $(^{-}7, 5)$ (f) $(7, {}^{-}2)$
(g) $(^{-}3, 7)$ (h) $(^{-}7, {}^{-}7)$ (i) $(1, {}^{-}2)$

p 24

A1
$0 \rightarrow {}^{-}6 \rightarrow 2 \rightarrow {}^{-}2 \rightarrow 7 \rightarrow$
$0 \rightarrow {}^{-}5 \rightarrow 3 \rightarrow {}^{-}3 \rightarrow {}^{-}5 \rightarrow$
$^{-}1 \rightarrow {}^{-}7 \rightarrow 4 \rightarrow {}^{-}3 \rightarrow {}^{-}5 \rightarrow 2$

A2
$0 - 6 = {}^{-}6$
$^{-}6 + 8 = 2$
$2 - 4 = {}^{-}2$
$^{-}2 + 9 = 7$
$7 - 7 = 0$
$0 - 5 = {}^{-}5$
$^{-}5 + 8 = 3$
$3 - 6 = {}^{-}3$
$^{-}3 - 2 = {}^{-}5$
$^{-}5 + 4 = {}^{-}1$
$^{-}1 - 6 = {}^{-}7$
$^{-}7 + 11 = 4$
$4 - 7 = {}^{-}3$
$^{-}3 - 2 = {}^{-}5$
$^{-}5 + 7 = 2$

B
(a) $^{-}4$ (b) $^{-}4$ (c) $^{-}2$
(d) $^{-}2$ (e) $^{-}4$

p 25

C1
(a) 9 (b) 1 (c) 7 (d) $^{-}4$
(e) 9 (f) 1 (g) 11 (h) 0
(i) $^{-}2$ (j) 21 (k) $^{-}7$ (l) $^{-}5$

C2
(a) 1 (b) $^{-}9$ (c) $^{-}2$ (d) $^{-}7$
(e) 5 (f) $^{-}10$ (g) $^{-}10$ (h) $^{-}12$
(i) 2 (j) $^{-}17$ (k) $^{-}20$ (l) $^{-}6$

Now try this!

Total 3

0	$^{-}1$	4
5	1	$^{-}3$
$^{-}2$	3	2

Total $^{-}3$

$^{-}2$	$^{-}3$	2
3	$^{-}1$	$^{-}5$
$^{-}4$	1	0

Total $^{-}9$

$^{-}4$	$^{-}5$	0
1	$^{-}3$	$^{-}7$
$^{-}6$	$^{-}1$	$^{-}2$

p 26

A2
(a) 12 (b) 21 (c) 56
(d) 18 (e) 40 (f) 24
(g) 36 (h) 36 (i) 56

B
25 and 30 → 150
50 and 20 → 100
25 and 40 → 200
11 and 20 → 220
12 and 40 → 120
25 and 35 → 175
75 and 40 → 600
65 and 15 → 195
15 and 55 → 165
15 and 25 → 75
75 and 20 → 300

p 27

C2 2, 3, 5, 7, 11, 13, 17, 19, 23, 29, 31, 37, 41, 43, 47, 53, 59, 61, 67, 71, 73, 79, 83, 89, 97

Now try this!
Possible answers include:
$9 = 2 + 7$ $49 = 2 + 47$
$16 = 5 + 11$ $64 = 3 + 61$
$25 = 2 + 23$ $81 = 2 + 79$
$36 = 5 + 31$ $100 = 3 + 97$

p 28

A1

(a)

1	16
2	8
4	

(b)

1	24
2	12
3	8
4	6

(c)

1	36
2	18
3	12
4	9
6	

(d)

1	16
2	24
3	16
4	12
6	8

(e)

1	25
5	

(f)

1	42
2	21
3	14
6	7

(g)

1	17

(h)

1	49
7	

(i)

1	32
2	16
4	8

(j)

1	23

(k)

1	40
2	20
4	10
5	8

(l)

1	64
2	32
4	16
8	

A2 A square number has an odd number of factors.
A3 17 and 23
A4 Possible answers include: 2, 3, 5, 7, 11, 13

B

12

1	12
2	6
3	4

18

1	18
2	9
3	6

20

1	20
2	10
4	5

28

1	28
2	14
4	7

p 29

C1 (a) 8 (b) 12
(c) 16 (d) 16
(e) 2 (f) 4
(g) 4 (h) 2
(i) 4 (j) 5
(k) 6 (l) 2
(m) 4 (n) 1

C2 (a) $\frac{2}{3}$ (b) $\frac{3}{4}$ (c) $\frac{1}{2}$ (d) $\frac{2}{3}$
(e) $\frac{21}{20}$ (f) $\frac{9}{16}$ (g) $\frac{10}{7}$ (h) $\frac{9}{32}$

Now try this!
(a) 1 (b) 96 (c) 96

p 30

A1 (a) 9 (b) 15
(c) 18 (d) 24
(e) 3 (f) 21
The sum of the digits is a multiple of 3.

A2 (a) 18 (b) 27
(c) 18 (d) 18
(e) 9 (f) 27
The sum of the digits is a multiple of 9.

B
124 → 2, 4
341 → no factors
5798 → 2
6714 → 2, 3, 6, 9
7920 → 2, 3, 4, 5, 6, 8, 9, 10
1584 → 2, 3, 4, 6, 8, 9
9458 → 2
2481 → 3
4570 → 2, 5, 10
36 819 → 3, 9
13 842 → 2, 3, 6, 9,
12 455 → 5
27 058 → 2
25 490 → 2, 5, 10
406 012 → 2, 4
462 124 → 2, 4
901 080 → 2, 3, 4, 5, 6, 8, 9, 10

p 31

Now try this!
(a) 40 (b) 60 (c) 360

p 32

A1 1, 4, 9, 16, 25, 36, 49
A2 64, 81, 100, 121, 144
A3 3, 5, 7, 9, 11, 13, 15, 17
They are consecutive odd numbers.
A4 1, 3, 6, 10, 15, 21, 28
A5 36, 45, 55, 66, 78
A6 2, 3, 4, 5, 6, 7, 8, 9
They are consecutive numbers.
A7 4, 9, 16, 25, 36, 49, 64, 81
They are consecutive square numbers.

p 33

C1 (a) 4 (b) 6
(c) 8 (d) 7
(e) 10 (f) 12
(g) 40 (h) 50
(i) 300

C2 (a) $\sqrt{16} = 4$ (b) $\sqrt{36} = 6$ (c) $\sqrt{64} = 8$
(d) $\sqrt{49} = 7$ (e) $\sqrt{100} = 10$ (f) $\sqrt{144} = 12$
(g) $\sqrt{1600} = 40$ (h) $\sqrt{2500} = 50$ (i) $\sqrt{90\,000} = 300$

C3

1: 2	4	2: 8	(shaded)	3: 9
9	(shaded)	0	(shaded)	0
4: 8	5: 4	3	6: 3	(shaded)
(shaded)	0	(shaded)	7: 8	5
8: 9	0	2	1	(shaded)

Now try this!
Possible answers include:

$3^2 = 9$ $\sqrt{9} = 3$ $10^2 = 100$ $\sqrt{100} = 10$
$9^2 = 81$ $\sqrt{81} = 9$ $1^2 = 1$ $\sqrt{1} = 1$
$13^2 = 169$ $\sqrt{169} = 13$ $6^2 = 36$ $\sqrt{36} = 6$
$19^2 = 361$ $\sqrt{361} = 9$ $31^2 = 961$ $\sqrt{961} = 31$
$301^2 = 90\,601$ $\sqrt{90\,601} = 301$
$603^2 = 363\,609$ $\sqrt{363\,609} = 603$

and all multiples of 10/100 of these, for example:
$30^2 = 900$ $\sqrt{900} = 30$

p 34

A1 (a) $\frac{1}{8}$ (b) $\frac{1}{3}$ (c) $\frac{2}{3}$
(d) $\frac{1}{6}$ (e) $\frac{5}{6}$ (f) $\frac{4}{10}$
(g) $\frac{5}{12}$ (h) $\frac{11}{12}$ (i) $\frac{7}{10}$

A2 $\frac{1}{8}$ $\frac{1}{6}$ $\frac{1}{3}$ $\frac{4}{10}$ $\frac{5}{12}$ $\frac{2}{3}$ $\frac{7}{10}$ $\frac{5}{6}$ $\frac{11}{12}$

A3 (a) $\frac{1}{4}$ (b) $\frac{1}{3}$ (c) $\frac{1}{2}$ (d) $\frac{1}{6}$
(e) $\frac{2}{3}$ (f) $\frac{3}{4}$ (g) $\frac{1}{12}$ (h) $\frac{5}{6}$
(i) $\frac{5}{6}$ (j) $\frac{5}{12}$ (k) $\frac{7}{12}$ (l) $\frac{1}{60}$

B Possible answers include:
4:20 pm and 4:55 pm 4:00 pm and 4:35 pm
4:05 pm and 4:40 pm 4:10 pm and 4:45 pm
4:15 pm and 4:50 pm 4:25 pm and 5:00 pm

p 35

C1 (a) $\frac{1}{3}$ (b) $\frac{5}{9}$ (c) $\frac{7}{9}$ (d) $\frac{8}{9}$
(e) $\frac{7}{9}$ (f) $\frac{2}{3}$ (g) $\frac{7}{9}$ (h) $\frac{7}{9}$

Now try this!
(a) $\frac{1}{2}$ (b) $\frac{1}{4}$ (c) $\frac{7}{24}$
(d) $\frac{1}{3}$ (e) $\frac{1}{8}$ (f) $\frac{7}{12}$
(g) $\frac{2}{3}$ (h) $\frac{3}{8}$ (i) $\frac{23}{24}$

p 37

C1 (a) $\frac{3}{5}$ N (b) $\frac{3}{10}$ B
(c) $\frac{3}{4}$ D (d) $\frac{1}{20}$ A
(e) $\frac{1}{10}$ M (f) $\frac{99}{100}$ M
(g) $\frac{1}{100}$ J (h) $\frac{9}{10}$ I
(i) $\frac{29}{100}$ S (j) $\frac{7}{20}$ O
(k) $\frac{1}{5}$ E (l) $\frac{19}{20}$ L
(m) $\frac{4}{5}$ F

C2 JAMES BOND FILM

p 38

A1 (a) $\frac{2}{5} < \frac{1}{2}$
(b) $\frac{5}{8} < \frac{3}{4}$
(c) $\frac{5}{6} < \frac{7}{8}$
(d) $\frac{4}{10} = \frac{2}{5}$
(e) $\frac{8}{10} > \frac{3}{4}$
(f) $\frac{2}{3} > \frac{5}{8}$

A2 $\frac{2}{3}$ $\frac{3}{5}$ $\frac{4}{6}$ $\frac{6}{10}$ $\frac{5}{8}$ $\frac{7}{8}$ $\frac{4}{5}$ $\frac{5}{6}$

B
$>$ $=$ $<$ $=$
$<$ $=$ $>$ $>$
$<$ $>$ $<$ $>$
$<$ $>$ $>$ $=$

p 39

C1 Smaller fractions:
(a) $\frac{3}{5}$
(b) $\frac{4}{5}$
(c) $\frac{3}{9}$

Now try this!
The proper fraction is always closer to 1 than the improper fraction.

p 40

A1 (a) ✗ 1 (b) ✔ (c) ✗ $1\frac{1}{5}$
(d) ✗ $1\frac{1}{2}$ (e) ✔ (f) ✔
(g) ✗ $1\frac{1}{8}$ (h) ✔ (i) ✗ $1\frac{3}{4}$
(j) ✔ (k) ✔ (l) ✗ $2\frac{1}{4}$
(m) ✔ (n) ✗ $2\frac{1}{8}$ (o) ✗ $2\frac{1}{6}$
(p) ✔ (q) ✔ (r) ✔

B ✔ x ✔ ✔
x ✔ ✔ ✔
x ✔ ✔ ✔

p 41

Now try this!

$\frac{2}{5}$	$\frac{3}{10}$	$\frac{4}{5}$
$\frac{9}{10}$	$\frac{1}{2}$	$\frac{1}{10}$
$\frac{1}{5}$	$\frac{7}{10}$	$\frac{3}{5}$

p 42

A1 (a) 6
(b) 8
(c) 12
(d) 6
(e) $\frac{4}{36}$ or $\frac{1}{9}$

A2 (a) 9
(b) 20
(c) 36
(d) 12
(e) 8
(f) $\frac{1}{18}$

A3 (a) 56
(b) 16
(c) 24
(d) 32
(e) 12
(f) 84

B (a) 24 (b) 15 (c) 35
(d) 20 (e) 35 (f) 49
(g) 40 (h) 60 (i) 33

p 43

C1 (b) The finish number is always six times smaller than the start number.

C2 (b) The finish number is always half the start number.

p 44

A1 $1\frac{1}{2}$ $1\frac{3}{5}$ $2\frac{1}{4}$ $2\frac{1}{2}$ $1\frac{3}{10}$ $2\frac{7}{10}$ $2\frac{1}{5}$ $1\frac{5}{8}$ $3\frac{1}{5}$ $3\frac{1}{2}$ $2\frac{1}{3}$ $3\frac{1}{8}$
$3\frac{4}{5}$ $4\frac{1}{4}$ 7 $2\frac{7}{8}$ $4\frac{2}{5}$ $1\frac{7}{8}$ $3\frac{1}{6}$ $3\frac{1}{2}$ $3\frac{3}{8}$ $3\frac{4}{9}$ $5\frac{2}{3}$ $2\frac{5}{7}$

B $6 \div 4$ $6 \times \frac{1}{4}$ Answer $1\frac{1}{2}$
$\frac{2}{5}$ of 10 $10 \div 5 \times 2$ Answer 4
$\frac{4}{5}$ of 2 $2 \times \frac{4}{5}$ Answer $1\frac{3}{5}$
$\frac{1}{3}$ of 6 $6 \times \frac{1}{3}$ Answer 2
$3 \div 4 \times 3$ $3 \times \frac{3}{4}$ Answer $2\frac{1}{4}$

p 45

C (a) $2\frac{1}{2}$ (b) 2 (c) 3
(d) $3\frac{1}{3}$ (e) $1\frac{1}{5}$ (f) $2\frac{2}{5}$
(g) $1\frac{1}{5}$ (h) $1\frac{3}{5}$ (i) $1\frac{7}{8}$
(j) $2\frac{2}{3}$ (k) $1\frac{3}{5}$ (l) $1\frac{7}{8}$

p 46

A3 (a) 0.3 (b) $\frac{3}{4}$ (c) 10%
(d) 97% (e) $\frac{1}{5}$ (f) $\frac{4}{5}$

B (a) 40% 0.4 $\frac{2}{5}$ (b) 70% 0.7 $\frac{7}{10}$
(c) 10% 0.1 $\frac{1}{10}$ (d) 80% 0.8 $\frac{4}{5}$
(e) 25% 0.25 $\frac{1}{4}$ (f) 97% 0.97 $\frac{97}{100}$
(g) 5% 0.05 $\frac{1}{20}$ (h) 75% 0.75 $\frac{3}{4}$
(i) 1% 0.01 $\frac{1}{100}$

p 47

C1 (a) 0.85 $\frac{17}{20}$ (b) 0.6 $\frac{3}{5}$
(c) 0.68 $\frac{17}{25}$ (d) 0.12 $\frac{3}{25}$
(e) 0.1 $\frac{1}{10}$ (f) 0.32 $\frac{8}{25}$
(g) 0.94 $\frac{47}{50}$ (h) 0.15 $\frac{3}{20}$
(i) 0.19 $\frac{19}{100}$ (j) 0.05 $\frac{1}{20}$
(k) 0.03 $\frac{3}{100}$ (l) 0.04 $\frac{1}{25}$

C2 (a) $\frac{1}{100} = 0.01$ (b) $\frac{1}{50} = 0.02$ (c) $\frac{3}{50} = 0.06$
(d) $\frac{17}{100} = 0.17$ (e) $\frac{7}{20} = 0.35$ (f) $\frac{24}{25} = 0.96$

Now try this!

			98%
20%	30%	31%	81%
6%	25%	20%	51%
42%	50%	15%	107%
68%	105%	66%	60%

p 48

A1 (a) 36 (b) 9 (c) 42 (d) 90
(e) 63 (f) 150 (g) 108 (h) 7.5

A2 (a) 6 (b) 9 (c) 105 (d) 18
(e) 45 (f) 22.5 (g) 13.5 (h) 2.1

p 50

A (a) £1295 (b) £348 (c) £1722
(d) £3869 (e) £4623 (f) £3984
(g) £7.80 (h) £13.80 (i) £254.80

B (a) £21.15 (b) £21.17 (c) £11.48
(d) £11.20 (e) £67.20 (f) £39.33

p 51

C1 (a) £7.04
(b) £4.23
(c) £5.10
(d) £2.97
(e) £4.50
(f) £7.28
(g) £7.05
(h) £6.75

C2 Boots

Now try this!
Rope £20
Torch £9

p 52

A1 (a) 24% (b) 46% (c) 31% (d) 75%
(e) 40% (f) 14% (g) 6% (h) 11%

A2 (a) 60% (b) 20% (c) 50%

B (a) 50% (b) 10%
(c) 25% (d) 75%
(e) 40% (f) 5%

p 53

C1 Estimates approximately:
(a) 30% (b) 70%
(c) 10% (d) 80%
(e) 60% (f) 40%

C2 Check that the pupils' estimates total 100%.
Estimates approximately:
(a) 5%, 20%, 25%, 50%
(b) 12.5%, 12.5%, 17%, 25%, 33%

Now try this!
34%

p 54

A1

Cheese pie	Sweet pastries
40 g flour 50 g butter 30 g cheese 100 ml milk	84 g sugar 70 g flour 6 g jam 2 eggs

Spinach parcels	Lemon cake
82 g flour 2 eggs 60 ml water 78 g spinach	1 lemon 90 g sugar 92 g flour 52 g butter

A2 (a) 5 (b) 10
(c) 15 (d) 20
(e) 25 (f) 30
(g) 35 (h) 40

B (a) €12.50 (b) €6.25
(c) €3.75 (d) €8.75
(e) €11.25 (f) €13.75

p 55

C1 (a) Lamb kebabs
(b) €13.35
(c) €6
(d) €7.08 (e) €11.85
(f) €5.25 (g) €10.65
(h) €14.75 (i) €24.85

C2 No

Now try this!
£3.56
£1.60
£1.89
£3.16
£2.36
£1.40
£2.84

p 56

A Beads shaded as follows:
(a) 1 grey bead
(b) 5 grey beads
(c) 2 grey beads
(d) 3 grey beads
(e) 10 grey beads
(f) 1 grey bead
(g) 7 grey beads
(h) 2 grey beads
(i) 4 grey beads
(j) 8 grey beads
(k) 6 grey beads

B1 (a) 3 : 1
(b) 1 : 3
(c) $\frac{3}{4}$
(d) $\frac{1}{4}$
(e) 25%
(f) 75%

B2 Possible statements include:
The ratio of white to grey beads is 4 : 1.
The ratio of grey to white beads is 1 : 4.
The proportion of grey beads is 20%.
The proportion of white beads is 80%.

p 57

C1 (a) $\frac{1}{2}$ 0.5 50% (b) $\frac{7}{10}$ 0.7 70%
(c) $\frac{1}{4}$ 0.25 25% (d) $\frac{2}{5}$ 0.4 40%
(e) $\frac{1}{10}$ 0.1 10% (f) $\frac{1}{5}$ 0.2 20%
(g) $\frac{3}{5}$ 0.6 60% (h) $\frac{3}{10}$ 0.3 30%

C2 (a) 1 : 1 (b) 7 : 3 (c) 1 : 3 (d) 2 : 3
(e) 1 : 9 (f) 1 : 4 (g) 3 : 2 (h) 3 : 7

Now try this!
(a) $\frac{1}{12}$
(b) 1 : 5
(c) 5 : 6

p 58

A1 21
A2 3
A3 8
A4 20
A5 16

B1 15 males 9 females
B2 10 males 25 females
B3 8 males 16 females
B4 20 males 35 females

p 59

C1 2000
C2 36
C3 12, 27
C4 £6000, £8000
C5 16
C6 9 kg, 15 kg

Now try this!
(a) £20 £15 £10
(b) 15 l 10 l 5 l
(c) £42 £77 £56